Starting from Scratch

D1264683

Recent Titles in
Libraries Unlimited Professional Guides for Young Adult Librarians
C. Allen Nichols and Mary Anne Nichols, Series Editors

The Teen-Centered Book Club: Readers into Leaders
Bonnie Kunzel and Constance Hardesty

Teen Programs with Punch: A Month-by-Month Guide
Valerie A. Ott

Serving Young Teens and 'Tweens
Sheila B. Anderson, editor

The Guy-Friendly Teen Library: Serving Male Teens
Rollie Welch

Serving Urban Teens
Paula Brehm-Heeger

The Teen-Centered Writing Club: Bringing Teens and Words Together
Constance Hardesty

More Than MySpace: Teens, Librarians, and Social Networking
Robyn Lupa, Editor

Visual Media for Teens: Creating and Using a Teen-Centered Film Collection
Jane Halsall and R. William Edminster

Teen-Centered Library Service: Putting Youth Participation into Practice
Diane P. Tuccillo

Booktalking with Teens
Kristine Mahood

Make Room for Teens!: Reflections on Developing Teen Spaces in Libraries
Michael G. Farrelly

Teens, Libraries, and Social Networking: What Librarians Need to Know
Denise E. Agosto and June Abbas, Editors

STARTING FROM SCRATCH

Building a Teen Library Program

Sarah Ludwig

Libraries Unlimited Professional Guides for Young Adult Librarians
C. Allen Nichols and Mary Anne Nichols, Series Editors

LIBRARIES UNLIMITED

AN IMPRINT OF ABC-CLIO, LLC
Santa Barbara, California • Denver, Colorado • Oxford, England

Library of Congress Cataloging-in-Publication Data

Ludwig, Sarah.
Starting from scratch : building a teen library program / Sarah Ludwig.
   p. cm. — (Libraries unlimited professional guides for young adult
librarians)
   Includes bibliographical references and index.
   ISBN 978-1-59884-607-2 (pbk. : acid-free paper) — ISBN 978-1-59884-608-9
(ebook)   1. Young adults' libraries—United States—Administration.
2. Libraries and teenagers—United States.   3. Young adult services
librarians—United States.   I. Title.
   Z718.5.L83 2011
   027.62′6—dc23   2011020103

ISBN: 978-1-59884-607-2
EISBN: 978-1-59884-608-9

15   14   13   12   11   1   2   3   4   5

This book is also available on the World Wide Web as an eBook.
Visit www.abc-clio.com for details.

Libraries Unlimited
An Imprint of ABC-CLIO, LLC

ABC-CLIO, LLC
130 Cremona Drive, P.O. Box 1911
Santa Barbara, California 93116-1911

This book is printed on acid-free paper ∞

Manufactured in the United States of America

To Evie

CONTENTS

Series Foreword   xi
Acknowledgments   xiii

Introduction   1
    Why Go into Teen Services?   1
    Getting a Job   5
    Why Teen Librarians Are Important   8
    Online Resources   14

1   Settling In   17
    Policies and Administration   17
    How Do You Fit In?   21
    Getting Help   24

2   Setting Up the Teen Space   29
    Display Furniture   31
    Rules for the Teen Space   32

3   Collection   39
    The Collection Development Policy   39
    Evaluating What You Already Have   41

The Core Collection   43
Digging Deeper   45
New Media   46
Organizing Your Collection   53
Ongoing Selection Tools   54
Knowing Your Readers and Your Community   58
The Reluctant Reader   60
Homework Collections: Yea or Nay?   63
Promoting the Collection   66
Obstacles in Collection Development   69

4   Programming   81
    Programming Ideas   82
    Summer Reading   98
    Community Programming   103
    What to Do When No One Comes   104
    Budget Constraints   106
    Advocating for Teen Programming   109

5   The Teen Advisory Board   113
    Recruiting Members   113
    Structure   114
    Responsibilities   115
    Activities   117
    Other Ways to Involve Teens   117

6   Outreach   121
    Introducing Yourself   121
    Social Networking   125
    Other Forms of Virtual Outreach   129
    Going into the Schools   131
    Other Community Partnerships   137
    Press   140
    Challenges with Outreach   143

7   Budget   149
    Getting Your Bearings   149
    Where Will the Money Go?   150
    Advocating for Your Program   151
    The Budget Proposal   157
    End of the Year Analysis   160

	Sources of Funding	164
	Budget Challenges	167
8	**Professional Development**	171
	Library Organizations	171
	Online Resources	173
	Continuing Education	182
	Conferences	185
	Networking/Getting Involved	189
	Career Growth: Where Do You Go from Here?	194
	Stress and Time Management	196
	Index	201

SERIES FOREWORD

We firmly believe that teens deserve distinct and diverse library services. They also should be provided equal access to library services and those services should be equal to those offered to other library customers. The wide array of titles in this series supports these beliefs. We are very excited about *Starting from Scratch* as the newest addition to our series. Many teen librarians may find the task of adding new service as daunting, but Sarah Ludwig has provided a valuable resource with a sensible and practical approach that gets the job done.

We are proud of our association with Libraries Unlimited/ABC-CLIO, which continues to prove itself as the premier publisher of books to help library staff serve teens. This series has succeeded because our authors know the needs of those library employees who work with young adults. Without exception, they have written useful and practical handbooks for library staff.

We hope you find this book, as well as our entire series, to be informative, providing you with valuable ideas as you serve teens and that this work will further inspire you to do great things to make teens welcome in your library. If you have an idea for a title that could be added to our series, or would like to submit a book proposal, please e-mail us at lu-books@lu.com. We'd love to hear from you.

Mary Anne Nichols
C. Allen Nichols

ACKNOWLEDGMENTS

I would not have had the opportunity to write this book were it not for my mentor and friend, Linda Braun, whom I met when I was her student at Simmons in 2003. Not only did Linda inspire me to become a teen librarian, she also invited me to write for the Young Adult Library Services Association blog, which put me in touch with the very kind C. Allen Nichols of Libraries Unlimited.

In my short career, I have had the great pleasure of working with many wonderful librarians and library staff. Some of those who mean the most to me are those with whom I worked so closely in the teen and technology department at Darien Library: Alex Hylton, Heather Martyn, Erica Leone, and Judy Sgammato. I also could not imagine life without my dear friend and former colleague, Kate Sheehan, who is one of the smartest people I know and who always offers brilliant advice.

Thanks, too, to all the people who have cheered me on throughout this process: my current boss, Lorri Carroll; my friends Gretchen Caserotti, Polly Alida Farrington, MK Eagle, and Abby Kracov Sesselberg; and the entire reference staff at Darien Library: Sally Ijams, Blanche Parker, Erica Bess, and Janet Davis.

There have been so many special students and teens in my professional life that it would be impossible to single any of them out. But it is because of them that I have such a deep and abiding love for my career. I am moved and inspired by my students every day. Working with children and teens is a gift, and I feel extraordinarily lucky to be in this field.

Finally, of course, I must say thank you to my parents, who gave me the gift of libraries and reading; my brother, for being my brother; and my husband, who is my champion in all situations. I love all of you. And thank you, Evie, for being a good sleeper and letting me write. You are the best girl a mom could ever hope for.

INTRODUCTION

WHY GO INTO TEEN SERVICES?

When I started my graduate program, like many library students before me, I wanted to be an academic librarian. It was a nice picture in my naïve mind: a book-lined office, bright-eyed college students asking me intellectually challenging research questions, tweed suits. I did enjoy my research classes, but as soon as I took young adult literature, I was hooked. It started out when I thought back on the books I'd read as a teen, and it grew when I read contemporary teen novels. I learned how important young adult literature can be to teens—how it can speak to teens who feel like no one else out there is like them. And from there, I started thinking about how important the *library* can be to teens.

So let's talk about that for a second. Why should libraries care about teens? Why would teens care about the library? When you were a teenager, did you spend a lot of time in the library? To be honest: I didn't. The public library of my teenage years was not my preferred hang-out spot. I was reading adult books—most library programs were geared toward children—and I preferred to spend my time doing school activities with my friends. But the library of my teenage years was not the library of my adult, professional years. Full disclosure: that library of years past was, in fact, run by my mother, who was the library director until I was in college. But I think even she would admit that, in the nineties, teen services were just starting to be discussed, and teens were a service group that were just starting to get cared about. I do remember, in middle school, a very cool young librarian who took an interest in my friends and me. We were desperate to impress her. She was a children's librarian, but she was responsible for the young adult collection, and I think she probably would have made a great teen librarian, had such a thing existed. I'm not saying that teen librarians are only good if they are regarded as cool and people to be impressed—but I am saying that librarians make or break the library experience for teens. Teens, who are so focused on relationships, good and bad—with their teachers, their boyfriends and girlfriends, their families, their coaches, their friends—respond to people.

If you have gone into teen services, then, congratulations and best wishes. You have the opportunity to have an enormous positive impact on young people's lives. Not all teens will love you—to some, you will be an annoyance, a nerd, a boring adult. To others, you will be a safe haven, a mentor, a role model, a trusted advisor. Whether you're funny, dorky, alt, dark, open, kind—whatever you are, however you present yourself—who you are is most important. And if you have a true desire to work with teens, then you have joined the right profession. I have found my work with teens to be often frustrating and more often incredibly satisfying. Teens are funny, sweet, insightful, generous, and honest. And they are also frequently misunderstood.

How many times have you heard an adult complain about teen behavior that is tolerated in other adults? How many times have you heard someone express nervousness at approaching a group of teenagers? How many times have you seen adults shoot giggling teens dirty looks? I'm not just talking about librarians here, although I'm sure we have all known librarians who have exhibited some of the above behavior. Why is this? We've all been teenagers before. We all remember what a difficult time it can be. And yet, it's as though once those years are over, as soon as we can say that we are adults, we want to remove ourselves so completely from adolescence that we lose all empathy for teens. We lump them together, stereotype, and avoid. And let's do talk about libraries, those community centers, those providers of open information to all. Where do teens fit into all that? Are they noisemakers to be shushed, skateboarders to be banned, gum chewers to reprimanded, or are they patrons like any other—patrons who have to follow the same rules as all of the other patrons, but patrons who at the same time deserve all of the same services as adults and children.

Teen librarians are teen advocates. We are the staff member who can push for expanded teen services, encourage our colleagues to go easy on the gum chewers, and give teens a voice. There are allies in every library—from circulation clerks to reference librarians to board members—who believe in the importance of teen services. But there are still those who are not comfortable with teens in the library. If you have been hired as a teen librarian, then your library has made a commitment to teen services, and that is a *huge* step in the right direction. Some of the best libraries in the country have not yet or have only recently hired teen librarians. Other libraries are shining examples of what teen services can be. I will list some of them in the Professional Development section, as they are programs to look to for inspiration and ideas.

Why Should You Care What I Think?

I am not an expert, but I have been in your position—in some ways I still am. I got my master's in library science in 2005 after about two years spent at Simmons College Graduate School of Library and Information Science. I attended all of my classes on the Mount Holyoke, or west campus, which is also where I happened to get my undergraduate degree in English and history. Almost immediately after graduating, I took a job at Wilbraham & Monson Academy, a small boarding school in western Massachusetts. I was extremely lucky to get this job so soon, and I started off in over my head. As the only MLS in the library, I had to learn how to do everything on my own, from how to budget to how to teach information literacy. Many of these lessons are present in this book. I am currently the Academic Technology Coordinator at Hamden Hall Country Day school, an independent school in the New Haven area, where I work with students of all ages in integrating technology into the curriculum. But the greatest influence that has led to the writing of this book was the two years I spent developing a teen program at a public library.

In 2008, I was hired by the Darien Library in Darien, Connecticut. The town was building a new library with a new teen space, and surprisingly, this innovative and forward-thinking institution had never employed a teen librarian. I was given the task of creating a teen department. I had no part in planning the physical space, but I did get to make furniture recommendations. When I started, we were still in the old library and I shared an office—literally, a closet—with my friend and colleague, Gretchen Caserotti, who is the Head of Children's Services at the library. Two weeks after my first day, I went into labor, and I did not return full-time to work until my daughter was six months old. I tell you this to illustrate how I started a new teen program on the opening day of a new library. I had the following: a collection of about 3,000 books; four computers; some armchairs rescued from the old building; and $15,000. Additionally, I was able to hire two part-time staff members in January of that year, to divide their time between the technology services department (which I had been made the head of as well) and the teen department. Combined, they had 38 hours per week in the library.

Eighteen months later, the teen department at Darien Library still had about 3,000 books. The space gained two computers, a flat-screen TV, and three video game consoles. Not much had physically changed. But here's what else the space had: the glass walls were covered in brightly colored adolescent handwriting. Teens were checking out about 1,500 books a month. About 300 teens a month attended programs, roughly four a week. Every day after school, every chair was filled, every computer was in use, and every game controller was in someone's hands. Successful programs included college admissions seminars, writing competitions, homework-help sessions, and art workshops. Teens were creating impromptu videos on Flip cameras, recording a monthly podcast, and tutoring senior citizens on using computers. The Teen Advisory Board hosted a talent competition attended by 160 teens and their families. The library stayed open late during high school exam periods to accommodate studiers.

I outline these successes not to toot my own horn, but to show you that success is possible in a reasonable period of time. Of course, I could not have done any of this without the support of my administration, colleagues, former classmates, and fellow teen librarians all over the country whose writing, presentations, and blog posts have been the reason for any success I've experienced. And I have experienced a vast number of failures. Programs that no one comes to, contests that no one enters, books that no one checks out, teens who openly mock me, parents who get angry at me, teens who never come in, theft, vandalism, bullying, porn—you name it. No job is perfect, no library is perfect, no librarian is perfect, no teen is perfect. But as you experience these successes and failures, know that you are not alone in your challenges, frustrations, and achievements. There are new professionals all over the country doing similar work. I hope that you can take solace in that and also see it as a recommendation to reach out. Don't isolate yourself, and don't try to do it all on your own. I hope that you find this book a useful tool in creating a new teen program. Best of luck. You will be amazing.

bly looking for someone who has a genuine interest in engag-
, in the library. Perhaps you are one of those people who was
in another area of the library and was hand-picked to work in
department—chances are, that's because of your personality and
oyment of being around teenagers. Showing potential employers
u adore teens could go a long way toward making you stand out
pplicant pool. And be specific: what is it, exactly, that appeals to
ut working with this age group? Is it their sense of humor? Their
y about the world? Their surprising ability to be kind, sensitive,
en-minded? Make sure this is clear in how you present yourself.
ecifics will show how genuine you are.

s on innovation. I do think you have to be cautious about promoting
rticular quality of yours, depending on the kind of library you're try-
work for. Some libraries are really pushing the boundaries of librarian-
nd public service, while others are still nervous about major change. If
ave been able to research a potential place of employment, you should
sense of how much the library values innovation, creativity, and a
on the new (and sometimes scary) versus the traditional and comfort-
If you are open to new ideas, want to learn, and are forward-thinking,
should always make this clear about yourself; it's just a matter of how
h emphasis you put on this quality and how out there you want to be. If
are going to be joining a more traditional library, you will still be able to
rk on those creative ideas of yours. One of the first things we learn on the
is how to work most effectively within the organization. And even the
st innovative of libraries do not accept innovation simply at face value.
Teamwork. It's a rare organization, library or otherwise, that does not
ructure its employees within teams—either formally or informally. It's
sy to think that you might be isolated and independent if you're going
be the only teen librarian (or, even more so, if you will be the only
brarian at all, in the case of many school librarians). But even if you are
solated in some ways, as in your job title, you will most likely be expected
o work in groups. School librarians sit on faculty committees and often
oin an academic department. Teen librarians in a public library will need
to collaborate constantly with their coworkers and managers. An interest
in and willingness to cooperate with, share ideas, and support your colleagues is considered a strength by many administrators.

WHY TEEN LIBRARIANS ARE IMPORTANT

I touched on this in my opening remarks. Teen librarians are valuable
advocates for teens, not just as library users but also as people. There are

GETTING A JOB

It's easy to get excited in graduate school. Maybe you loved one of
your professors or one of your classes—loved talking about how important teen librarians are, or about all the cool things you're going to do in
your first job. Or maybe you already have a job at a library, doing something else, either as a librarian or a nonprofessional staff member. Either
way, once school is over, it's time to start working. And in this economic
climate, that can be a challenge. But in this economic climate, libraries
are more important than ever—so keep at it. Here are some things to
think about.

Don't discount the job that's not exactly what you were looking for. We all
have a picture in our head of our dream job. For me, right out of Simmons,
it was a position in an urban public library. Instead, I worked at a small
suburban boarding school for three years. Instead of spending three years
wishing I was somewhere else, I learned almost everything I now know
about teen services, in addition to forming lasting connections with teens.
Had I passed that opportunity up in order to hold out for my dream job, I
would have been doing myself a disservice. Yes, this is anecdotal evidence,
but I do encourage you to search broadly and remain open-minded. Interviews are a wonderful opportunity to learn more about a specific position,
the workplace, and whether or not your interests and skills will apply to a
position you might not have expected to pursue.

*Get any job in a library while you're still in school . . . or even if you've already
graduated.* If you're reading this before graduation, it's a great idea to start
working in a library in some capacity before you're ready to go for a professional position. Volunteering can do the trick if you can afford it. It
gives you real-world experience that you can put on your resume, plus it's
putting you in contact with librarians who might have job leads, either at
the library where you're working or elsewhere. And while it's not the best
financial solution, a part-time or non-professional job might be your way
in even after you've earned your MLS.

Use the human resources you've got. Your professors have connections.
Your classmates might already work in libraries or schools. Ask around,
get MOO mini business cards to pass to your classmates, and ask your
professors to write you letters of recommendation to keep on file.

Start somewhere. Some libraries don't have full-time young adult (YA)
positions. But some libraries *do* have reference librarians who work with
teens for a few hours a week. If you feel like you're up to the challenge,
it could be worth taking a position where you're with teens a certain

percentage of your day, and then using those fantastic advocacy skills of yours to push for a full-time teen program…that you would manage, of course!

Think about relocating. This is dependent on your life situation, of course, but some states always seem to have job openings posted in *American Libraries,* while others never do. If you can move to work a great job, do it!

Use technology to stay on top of things. You can subscribe to RSS feeds on most job search sites. Visiting your feed reader every day can keep you up-to-date on all the new jobs that have been listed since the last time you looked. Indeed.com even allows you to subscribe to multiple custom searches that you create using keywords and location preferences. Libworm.com makes it easy to subscribe to lots of library-related feeds, including one just for job openings.

In terms of job hunting, there are loads of resources available to you, which, of course, can be incredibly overwhelming. Here are some that you should definitely keep an eye on.

- Libgig (www.libgig.com). Often, this website will list jobs that others don't, like positions in nontraditional libraries and for-profit organizations. They don't list many youth services openings, but it's still worth keeping an eye on the site.

- Simmons GSLIS Jobline (www.simmons.edu/gslis/careers/jobs/jobline/). If you're looking in New England, this is a great resource. Keep in mind that listings are posted weekly, so you have to click back through previous weeks to see all of the openings.

- LISjobs (www.lisjobs.com/). You can search through listings directly on the site, but there's also a fantastic section that lists job banks by state, including jobs at large libraries and via library consortiums and organizations.

- ALA Joblist (joblist.ala.org/). Posts mostly management and MLS jobs—you won't find many paraprofessional jobs here. Jobs from all over the country are posted. Some provide salary ranges.

- Employment Resources for Librarians (home.netcom.com/~feridun/nlintro.htm). A huge collection of job hunting resources—job banks, newspaper listings, career placement sites, recruiters and temp firms, and so on.

- UT School of Information JobWeb (www.ischool.utexas.edu/jobweb/Search.php). Another grad school site; unlike Simmons, this one posts jobs from all over the country, but it does tend to be heavy on jobs in Texas and the South.

Pitching Yourself: Th[...]
Already H[...]

When you're job hunting, it's easy to r[...] "I'm not qualified" and then, "How can I [...] the best idea, but to look at it in another v[...] what a potential employer is looking for? [...] your experience, you might realize that you[...] didn't think you had. Here are some that wi[...]

Comfort with technology. Not everyone has t[...] tech, but in order to work in today's library—[...] you need to at least feel comfortable learnin[...] technology. What are your interests? Do you fe[...] networks? What about blogging? Even having [...] that you're familiar with the medium. Have yo[...] you like to play computer or video games in you[...] you haven't done these things in a library settin[...] couldn't.

Interest in many areas of librarianship. Teen librar[...] responsive, and well-rounded. A day in the life [...] mean:

- Ordering books from a new list of recommend[...]
- Visiting the high school to speak to the journa[...] new writing program
- Planning a talent show
- Writing a press release
- Troubleshooting the videogame hookup in the tee[...]
- Sitting on the reference desk—and yes, answering [...] tions from people of *all* ages

The more you demonstrate that you are—genuinely, of c[...] in working in many areas of librarianship, the more you h[...] pay attention to what the specific job requirements are, a[...] even embellish, but emphasize that you are comfortable s[...] and taking on new tasks and responsibilities.

Love of teens. This is not so much a skill as it is a passion [...] say that *love* is too strong a word…but I disagree. Do you l[...] with teens? *Really* love it? Well, believe it or not, not everyon[...] library administrators who are planning on expanding servi[...]

issues that apply to teens that don't apply to other age groups, and there are adolescent needs that can be filled by a library—needs that other ages might not experience. What follows is a synopsis that does not do justice to the huge body of literature that exists to advocate for teen services. The American Library Association (ALA) and its division, the Young Adult Library Services Association (YALSA) have made it their mission to provide teen librarians with the tools they need to argue for teen programs, and they have many online resources that are available to you for free via their website. The end of this section contains a compilation of some of those resources.

Connecting Young Adults and Libraries

Teens deserve library services. That's a statement that not everyone might agree with. If librarians have had negative experiences with teens, and if teens haven't been library users in the past, then it's been easy for people to ignore and stereotype teens at your library up till now. Some adults will make the argument that teens don't like to read, or don't appreciate libraries, and therefore don't deserve them. In areas where there are lots of activities available to teens, you may hear people say that teens already have enough to do.

Teens grow up into adults. Adults support library services. Sometimes it's as simple as that. If you believe that libraries are vital to communities, then you must also know that libraries live or die by their communities. Why should we ever cease excellent services to one user group simply because they hit puberty, and then pick up with them again once they graduate from college? Teens were once children, and they will soon be adults. If we want everyone to love and support the library—with their checkbooks, their voices, or their votes—then we should consider the fact that library experiences make library supporters. Or they don't. Which side do we want our future adults on?

Of course there will always be teens who don't like being at the library no matter what you do, but there are several arguments to be made that teens do deserve libraries. Here are some basic talking points:

- Teens are equal members of your community. At the very least, you and your colleagues should fundamentally agree with this statement. No group should be denied library services based on age.
- Teens have unique needs that are different from adults' and children's. The library has an obligation to address those unique needs. See the next section for more detail about this point.

- If teens in your community do not have access to technology at home, then they rely on the library and their school to provide them with access to computers for personal and academic research, entertainment, and homework tools like word processing programs.

- If teens in your community struggle with literacy, then the library can have a positive impact on their lives by providing them with access to materials and services that have the potential to increase literacy of all types.

- The library helps keep teens safe by providing them with a place to spend time after school and on the weekends. By doing this, the library is providing a valuable service to the community and perpetuating a cycle of positive behavior among teens.

Teens Are Not Children

If you're already in a library doing something else, and if your library doesn't have a teen department, then you might want to consider making the case for the development of one. Many libraries serve teens through their children's department. Some libraries, as much as we hate to admit it, aren't thrilled by the idea of bringing more teens into the library. If they're already there, bothering the adult patrons, leaving food wrappers everywhere and tipping their chairs back on two legs, then the last thing librarians want to do is increase teen patron numbers.

Children's librarians are not teen librarians. That isn't to say that the children's librarians who serve teens aren't working hard, wholly committed, or philosophically in favor of service to teens. If a library wants to truly develop services to teens, then they must have a designated teen librarian. This person is responsible for building only the teen collection, developing only teen programs, advocating only for teens, marketing and reaching out only to teens.

I can't speak with a lot of authority about the responsibilities of children's librarians, since I'm not one, but I do know that, simply put, the developmental needs of teens are different than that of children. Here are some examples:

- Programming: A story time is not the same as an anti-prom. The goals for teen programming often center on filling a need or creating a space where teens feel comfortable expressing themselves, exploring ideas, or letting down their guard in ways they might not normally feel safe to do.

- Reader's Advisory: Certainly, young adult literature and children's literature both try to address the interests and curiosities of their audience, but young adult literature is not for most children. The social, personal, and familial issues that often arise in adolescence are addressed specifically in teen books. Librarians need to feel comfortable recommending appropriate reading materials, which means they have to read as much of it as they can.

- Research: Teens have different literacy and academic needs than children. They need help with MLA citations, college applications, job hunting, and primary sources. They're doing personal research on the issues that are important to them: sex, dating, music, family problems, substance abuse, fashion. They are exploring themselves and their surroundings in a way that many of us no longer have time for. And unlike children, who learn so much through the filters of the adults in their lives, teens have the freedom to explore on their own. They are hungry for knowledge. It just doesn't always look like research. Sometimes it's disguised as goofing off. But even a visit to YouTube can be an exploration.

Serving the Underserved

This is a phrase that you have perhaps heard before. "Serving the underserved" can relate to any number of population groups: Spanish speakers. Nontraditional families. New Americans. Seniors. Any group in your community that is not being served well can be considered underserved. As for what "served well" means, I don't have a great description. If you analyze the services that your library is providing, you can probably identify the user groups that are receiving the best. Perhaps it's school aged children, or senior citizens, or job seekers. Can you spot trends in the programming that your library provides? What audience do the library's databases best reach?

Some consider the underserved to be untapped markets. See, for example, Katherine Mossman's 2006 article, "Serving the Niche," in which she writes that "Libraries have traditionally reached underserved or underused markets by developing innovative programming in public libraries; bringing library services to any classroom or information commons; and, in academic libraries, stepping up efforts to reach out to university or college faculty members. We've also tapped an underworked market by implementing the now widespread use of digital reference services, or so-called 'virtual' reference services. We need to do more of this type of creative outreach."[1] There is a good chance that teens are an untapped market in your community. Do teens avoid the library because it has nothing to offer them—or if it does, they're unaware of it? Would they rather do other things like go to the mall, go home, or engage in risky behaviors? If the library has made a commitment to connect with potential library users who are not currently taking advantage of library services, then looking to teens may be a step in the right direction.

Why is serving the underserved a valuable undertaking for libraries? In all communities there are the privileged and the underprivileged. While I am of the belief that all people should have access to the library—and that all people should be able to find something for them at the library—there are certainly some groups who have more to gain from library services than others. In many cases, this gets back to access to technology. It may be hard for some of us to imagine, but there are many areas of the country in which the Internet is not available in people's homes. And we all know that not everyone can afford a computer. In this day and age, teens are asked more and more to show their technological competency at school. They have to create slideshows, multimedia presentations, and hand in typed assignments. Even beyond that, in order to stay connected with friends, teens need access to the Internet. And if teens want to learn more about themselves and their worlds, the Internet is the easiest way to do so in a private, self-controlled way. Technology can empower teens, and if teens do not have access to technology, they are at a disadvantage. In addition, we must go back to basics. Many households do not have books in them. If we want to get books into the hands of adolescents, then we need to get adolescents into the library. Many teens do not find constructive, healthy activities to do at home. The library can provide those things and more.

Literacy

In certain communities, literacy is not a huge issue, though certainly not all teens in high-literacy areas are avid readers or excel at reading comprehension. Teens who struggle with reading live in every community. In my state of Connecticut in 2009, 43 percent of eighth graders scored at or above reading proficiency. Once the population group expands nationwide, that number drops to 32 percent.[2] Delve into the specifics of surveys like this, and you will see how the numbers break down further—by economic status or gender, for example. We must avoid making blanket statements about groups, but we also must be aware of the challenges faced by some teens and the need to promote literacy with all adolescents.

The teen librarian plays an important role in promoting literacy, which is generally defined as "the ability to read, write, speak, and compute at a certain level."[3] So when you think about it, nearly everything the teen librarian does supports the growth of literacy skills. The librarian can plan programs that specifically address literacy, like writing groups, poetry competitions, open mic nights, rap battles, graphic novel classes, 30-second haiku programs, word games, or songwriting workshops. Books can be selected that are of interest to teens, which promotes reading. The library can post booklists on its website and link to literacy resources, like the Salt Lake City Library does: http://www.slcpl.lib.ut.us/details.jsp?parent_id=383&page_id=389.

A more in-depth program might offer writing instruction and homework help to teens. Libraries that offer after-school homework help often find themselves flooded with teens who want a space to spread out their books, eat snacks, get free school supplies, sit with their friends, and ask for help. If a significant number of people in your community speak English as a second language, the library can be a center for language learning classes, one-on-one instruction, and free access to databases and other electronic resources.

Perhaps most importantly, librarians promote literacy by making reading enjoyable. Reading is *fun,* not a chore, not something to feel pressure about. Rather, reading can be something to share with others or reflect on in private. And librarians promote literacy by promoting the library. No one learns by osmosis, but the library is a place of learning and sharing, and if teens are in the library, then they are in a place where reading, writing, and learning are made accessible, safe, and fun.

Increasingly, information literacy is becoming a demand of school and the workplace. Teens must be armed with the ability to sort through a massive amount of information in order to perform well in most situations, personal and academic. How does one develop information literacy skills? By having access to information in all its forms, and by learning how to evaluate and synthesize the information. This happens all the time whether we are aware of it or not, but the library is in a unique position to guide teens toward stronger information literacy skills. This happens every single day in the school library. In the public library, it happens less formally. Librarians help teens undergo independent learning by pointing them toward materials that are of interest to them. Librarians also assist with creating search strategies. Any time a teen comes in to work on a research assignment, we are able to work closely with them to introduce or reinforce these skills.

Developmental Assets

The Search Institute, a nonprofit organization "committed to helping create healthy communities for every young person,"[4] offers numerous resources for those who work with children and teens. Many librarians who work with adolescents have used the Search Institute's 40 Developmental Assets as a framework for how they provide services to teens. The assets can be found here: http://www.search-institute.org/content/40-developmental-assets-adolescents-ages-12–18. They are split into internal and external assets and address things like values, empowerment, support, and social competencies.

The Search Institute provides a service wherein it visits a community and conducts a survey of all students within certain grades—in many cases, grades 7 and 12—that address all of the 40 developmental assets. Once the results are in—and they are often surprising—community groups can decide how to respond to these results. Even if your community does not undertake a survey, you can still promote the developmental assets within your library and with others in your community who work with teens.

The reason, I think, why the developmental assets resonate so well with teen librarians is because we have a strong interest in promoting the health and well-being of teens. Because the assets are focused on community, positive role models, and adult support, the library easily is able to find itself a positive influence on teens' lives. After all, it is our job to be positive role models and support teens as they expand their horizons and satisfy their curiosities. Additionally, because the assets emphasize giving teens a voice, librarians can use this as justification for developing youth-centric programs like teen advisory boards, teen content creation, and teen-generated programming.

Much has been written about libraries and the developmental assets, so much so that it is difficult to summarize the connection. To read more about this topic, the Search Institute has information on its website at http://www.search-institute.org/librarians-0.

ONLINE RESOURCES

For more information about advocating for young adult services, try the following:

"Advocating for Teen Services in Libraries." http://wikis.ala.org/yalsa/index.php/Advocating_for_Teen_Services_in_Libraries. A list of online resources and some information about YALSA's Advocacy Campaign.

"Public Library Talking Points for Patrons Age 13–18." http://www.lita.org/ala/ issuesadvocacy/advocacy/advocacyuniversity/additup/13to18/ALA_ print_layout_1_523577_523577.cfm. Seven simple and clear reasons why teens need access to library professionals and resources.

"Speaking Up for Library Services to Teens" (PDF) http://www.ala.org/ala/ mgrps/divs/yalsa/advocacy_final.pdf. Prepared by YALSA for the Campaign for America's Libraries. Includes sample materials and further resources.

"The YA Advocacy Action Plan Workbook" (PDF) http://yalsa.ala.org/presen tations/AdvocacyWorkbook.pdf. A document generated by librarians at YALSA's Advocacy Preconference Institute in January 2008.

NOTES

1. Katherine Mossman, "Serving the Niche: Viewing Libraries through Chris Anderson's 'Long Tail' Lens," *Library Journal,* July 15, 2006, available at http:// www.libraryjournal.com/article/CA6349032.html.

2. Linda Conner Lambeck, "State Student Reading Scores Rise, but Many Still Fall Short," *Connecticut Post,* March 25, 2010, available at http://www.ctpost.com/ news/article/State-student-reading-scores-rise-but-many-still-420982.php.

3. Linda Schamber, "The Role of Libraries in Literacy Education," *LibraryIn struction.com,* 2003, available at http://www.libraryinstruction.com/literacy-education.html.

4. "About Us," *Search Institute,* available at http://www.search-institute.org/ about.

1

$\diamond \diamond \diamond$

SETTLING IN

Once you've arrived at your new library, you'll have to make some quick decisions about how you want your space to look and be managed, how you'd like to fit into the organization, and how you want your program to be run. It can be overwhelming. You don't have to make all of these decisions at once, but keep them in mind as you start to get a feel for your community and your library. The best way to prepare yourself is to familiarize yourself with the way your library is organized and managed and with the library's mission statement. Start there.

POLICIES AND ADMINISTRATION
The Teen Department Mission Statement

Most libraries have mission statements; not many have teen mission statements. The teen department's mission should be in line with the entire library's, but there are some advantages to having a statement that applies just to teen services. A mission statement guides all that you do. It provides a framework for services, policies, collection development, programming, and more. The exercise of writing a mission statement is often just as important as the finished product itself. If you do not have one, I would sit down with your staff and any other invested staff members—perhaps a representative from each department—and go through the effort of boiling down the teen department's mission into a few sentences. To get started, you will want to visit library websites to read what others have put together. Not all library mission statements can be found online, however, and some of those that are don't speak to teen services; it is worth calling area libraries, or libraries known for their high-quality teen programs, to see if they can share their mission statements with you.

Once you've been inspired by these examples, use these questions as a basis for your conversation:

1. What is the overall purpose of the teen department?
2. What are some important stories that we can tell about the teen department?
3. What is our product? In other words, what programs and services do we provide?
4. What makes the teen department different from other departments?
5. How does the teen department fit into the library?

The answers to these questions should result in a concise, clear, 2–5 sentence statement. Once you have drafted your mission statement and run it by your administration, continue talking to your staff about it and how it guides your services. Every year, look at the mission statement and see if your accomplishments over the past year reflect its sentiment, and plan goals for the coming year that use the mission statement as a guide. If you ever produce materials that outline general information about the teen department, you may want to make sure the mission statement is included.

Understanding Your Library's Policies

Simply put: you must be familiar with your library's policies. Public libraries often have policies that are very different from school libraries or from other libraries. In graduate school, you often will not learn about policies and how they can affect your work. You will find, however, that some libraries are entirely guided by policies and seem to have a rule for every situation, while others are much more lax and require staff to exercise good judgment. No matter what, read over the materials that your manager or human resources representative gives you. Read the policies posted on your library website. Ask questions about what you don't understand.

Public library policies usually center around patron behavior, use of public spaces, and use of technology. Patron behavior policies can address everything from noise to body odor to cell phone use. Technology use policies usually prohibit the use of computers to view inappropriate materials, though some libraries will allow this in some situations while others will not. And the use of public spaces is perhaps the trickiest of all. Libraries with rooms that are available for reservation have to be very careful about who can use their rooms, in order to avoid discriminating against any particular group. Another issue is allowing for-profit business representatives to use the space. Ask your administrators before you bring in a sales rep to run a program and put their logo all over the promotional materials—this could be a no-no.

Fostering Your Relationship with Library Administration

In general terms, fostering a relationship with the library administration means communicating like crazy. It is better to over-communicate than to find yourself in a bad situation that could have been avoided had you asked questions. If you have the desire to grow within the organization, or even to advocate for your department most effectively, you need to be present to the administrators. Set up regular meetings with your manager, and try to meet with the director on a regular basis, too. Bring them issues, questions, and successes. If you are not required to write a monthly report, write one anyway and include photos. Any time you are mentioned in the press, make sure that the director knows about it. (It is also a good idea to always let your director know if the press plans to attend an event or interview you—directors don't like to be surprised by these things, even if it is positive coverage.)

Your administrators are your allies. They brought you into the library and clearly value teen services. Teen departments are often not regarded as equal to adult and children's services, though—perhaps because they serve a smaller portion of the population—and it is your job to make sure that teen services is granted the same resources as other departments. This will only come about if you have a relationship with the administration that allows you to bring your success stories and challenges to them. If you start this from the very beginning, you will soon find yourself in a great position to advocate for your department.

Forming Relationships with Your Colleagues

No librarian works in a vacuum. You will absolutely come to rely on your colleagues, no matter how large or small your organization is. And when it comes to developing a program from its inception, you will need help from those you work with. Make sure you spend a significant amount of time meeting and getting to know your coworkers. Tell them how excited you are to collaborate with them and that you look forward to supporting them on anything they might need. As you start to talk with people, you will learn about their professional interests and goals, and you might start to see where the teen department fits into all that.

If you can find people on staff you're comfortable being open with, ask them to help you understand the organization and its subtleties. All libraries have...quirks. Hopefully, whoever hired you gave you a tour, put materials into your hands, and got you set up on a computer. Spend some time looking through everything you can, but also be sure to ask questions and find out how things work according to the staff.

Your fellow librarians will be able to tell you a great deal about the community and the teens that live in it. They may have ideas that you disagree with, but they also can give you insight into how teens have used the library (or not) thus far. They might know that you're in a big sports town, for example, or that teens in your neighborhood tend not to attend college after graduation. Ask about past conflicts with teens, past successes, whether anyone on staff has taken an interest in teens before now. And if anyone offers help, take it. You want to start out forming relationships. Just make sure that you are having frequent conversations with your manager, who may be able to fill you in on organization issues that make it difficult for your colleagues to lend you very much of their time. Some libraries are structured pretty rigidly, and staff may not have the flexibility to lend a hand on projects outside of their department.

A theme of this section is that teen librarians bridge the gap between children's and adult services, so it is wise to spend time talking with the heads of both departments. And not only is teen services a bridge, it is also a department that serves patrons who spend time in more areas of the library than any other group. After all, teens are in the teen area, the children's room, and the adult sections. You may find that your new coworkers are looking to you to deal with teens that thus far have been avoided. This is a good thing and a bad thing. It's good for you to be regarded as the expert on teens and to have the chance to interact with teens as much as possible. It's bad for other staff members to feel like they don't have to talk to teens. This fine line will be your responsibility, and if you are fortunate you will have the full support of your administration in acknowledging the balance. It will take some education on your part to make sure that all staff members know how to best approach teens—and that they don't think teens aren't their problem.

HOW DO YOU FIT IN?
Your Desk

If you work in a public library and you're lucky enough to have a whole teen room at your disposal, I recommend finding a space in that room for a staff desk, no matter how small. Some may argue that placing a desk in the teen room will make teens feel less comfortable, but I find that it's worse not to have a presence in the room. If there's no desk, then teens don't know where they should go to find help. They won't associate you with that space. And you won't have as much of a chance to get to know them. If you can't have a desk, get yourself into that room as much as possible. You'll meet kids when you run programs, but that's not enough. Be a presence after school and on the weekends, if you can. Shelving books is a great excuse to be in the teen room. Introducing yourself might make everyone feel a little awkward, but you'll soon get a sense of your teens and how much space they need.

When I visit other libraries, if the teen area is empty, there's never a librarian in sight. At libraries like ImaginOn at the Public Library of Charlotte & Mecklenburg County, the librarians are right smack dab in the middle of things. They're also, not coincidentally, surrounded by teens. Teens certainly need privacy, but I also think that a neglected space will eventually send the message that nobody at the library cares about it.

When I worked in a school library, I spent my first two years at the front desk. I greeted everyone who came in, and I was the first person they came to when they had a question. At the beginning of my third year, I made, in retrospect, a poor choice to switch with the library assistant and take the desk in the back office. After two years of my students thinking she was my boss, my pride overtook my good judgment. Fortunately, by then I'd formed enough of a relationship with our students to get by, but I should have stayed out front. The librarian should be on the front lines, available at all times to answer reference questions, joke around with students, and, frankly, keep an eye on things—if you overhear a student complaining about finding nothing to read, or lamenting a slow Internet connection, you are right there to help. The school librarian is the face of the library and as such should be as visible as possible. The demands of back office work make it difficult to be on the front lines at all times. But at least at the beginning, when you're trying to be as visible as possible, make as much of an effort as possible to stay out front: it's an easy way to be a presence in your students' lives.

How the Teen Librarian Fits into the Library

As I have already mentioned, the teen librarian bridges the gap between children's services and adult services. For this reason, you may find yourself working with many different people on staff. This is a good thing, but it can get complicated. When do kids start being teens? How does that affect your collection and your programming? When do teens start being adults? Where do college students belong? Talk to your colleagues and be open to their ideas. When a new teen program is being developed, you will have to make choices about age limits, and you can't make these decisions alone.

For this reason, teen librarians must maintain a visible presence in the library, constantly communicating with other librarians, especially those in the children's and reference departments. Go to their meetings if you can, and if there's a department head group at your school or library, go to that, too. It's your job to cheerlead teen programs and stand up for teens, and the only way to do that is to form relationships with your colleagues. If a teen program is attracting younger children, for example, it's good if you can brainstorm with the children's librarian—should the program be moved to a different department? Should you try to advertise it differently?

Teen librarians wear many hats. They plan programs, conduct reader's advisory and reference, market and advertise programs, develop outreach strategies, implement technology, and do all that fun administrative work—budgeting, staffing, acquisitions, and more. I spent the first year of my librarian life learning how to do all of the latter tasks. It's worth taking the time to do this before you put pressure on yourself to develop innovative programs and complicated initiatives. (And that's why I'll spend so much time on all this later on.)

Take cues from the teens themselves, if they're already coming into the library. When I was at Darien Library, the middle school students went into the teen lounge and the high school students went to the reference area, because it felt more collegiate. There was no reason for me to force anyone to change their behavior, but I did have to be aware of this when it came time to plan services and marketing.

The Philosophy That Guides Your Service: Youth Participation

Above all, the most successful teen programs are those that invite teen participation. This idea—that teens should have a voice both in teen services and in the library—should be the foundation of all of your choices for the department. Involving teens in the library means that they are not only having a positive impact on that institution, they are also having a positive impact on their community. As a youth leader, I believe it is your responsibility to help teens develop into kind, conscientious, responsible, and community-minded adolescents and adults. Despite what others might say, it is never too late—there isn't some magic age when children are done growing and changing. Teens, too, can be influenced by the adults in their lives.

The backbone of youth participation is the teen advisory board, which is described in great detail in Chapter 5. But more than specific programs and services, it should be clear to you, anyone else in your department, and your library colleagues that:

- The library cares about and values teens.
- Teens are important members of their community.
- Teens deserve quality library services.
- Teens deserve a voice in how the library provides services and information for them.
- Teen input will have a direct impact on how the library serves that age group.

Not everyone in the library will buy into this, and that's OK—and normal. But you need to. Your responsibility is to protect these beliefs and do whatever you can to make sure the library as an organization is behind them. Don't obsess over them, but when it comes to plan a major new initiative, or even a season of programming, do think about how youth participation might play into it. When you establish your goals for the department, find a way to relate them back to this philosophy. As long as you can keep it in your bearings, you'll ensure that you're doing the best you can to give teens room to grow, feel safe, and get the most they can out of the library.

For more information on youth participation and why it is so important to the development of young adults, I recommend the following resources:

- YALSA's Guidelines for Participation of Youth in Libraries contains a concise definition of youth participation and offers examples of

what it can look like in a library: http://www.infopeople.org/
training/past/2007/teen-programming/cg_YALSA_guidelines_
for_youth_participation.pdf

- Diane P. Tuccillo's *Teen-Centered Library Service: Putting Youth Participation into Practice* (Libraries Unlimited, 2009) is a guide to getting teens involved in the library as well as an exploration of why this is critical.

- Linda Braun's *Technically Involved: Technology-Based Youth Participation Activities for Your Library* (ALA Editions, 2003) is seven years old, but has excellent, timeless information about why youth participation is so important, as well as practical advice that is still applicable in 2011. It is available digitally via Google Books in nearly its entirety.

- To get more actively involved in this topic, join YALSA's Youth Participation Interest Group. For more information, visit this blog post, which includes information on how to join: http://yalsa.ala.org/blog/2010/04/10/youth-participation-interest-group/

GETTING HELP
Volunteers

Some libraries have established and well-attended volunteer programs already in place. School librarians may find that parents are either already volunteering or desperately want to. In either case, you can skip ahead past the recruitment step. In libraries where there is a sluggish or nonexistent volunteer base, you will need to speak to the person in charge of such things—perhaps that's the director—to see if the library will get behind a volunteer program.

Finding volunteers might be as easy as placing a notice on the library website. Other places to look and ask: in the schools (ask the administrative assistant whom to talk to); in the children's library (parents might want to help out; ask the librarians if they will post a sign for you somewhere in the children's library); at a meeting of the Parent Teacher Association; at a library board meeting; in the teen area itself. Ask parents who are picking up their children to help you spread the word. You could place an ad in the paper or send out an e-blast, or include a bookmark with every date-due slip.

A word about volunteers before we get into specific talks and responsibilities: volunteers cannot replace paid staff. Libraries cannot be entirely run by untrained, unpaid help. I mention this because in this age of budget cuts, some critics of libraries have suggested that a way to save money is to replace librarians with unpaid volunteers. I know I am preaching to the choir when I say that this is not possible. Librarians and nonprofessional staff are what make the library work. Without trained staff, the library would be nothing but an unorganized attic full of books. Along these lines, I would caution you not to bring in volunteers to do the work of librarians. It's not fair to the volunteer who is doing difficult, time-consuming work for free, and it's not fair to the paid staff to have their tasks done by an unpaid worker. That said, volunteers are not slave labor. They don't want to spend their time stamping hundreds of withdrawn books or alphabetizing books—certainly, you can give them tasks like this, but don't expect that they will do this for hours on end without wanting something a bit more interesting, or that feels more meaningful to the library.

So it's important to find a balance. I would think about volunteering in terms of projects. What tasks do you need to accomplish over the coming weeks? Can a volunteer help with the project? Or can they take on some of your tasks to free you up? Here are some sample daily tasks that you might consider giving to a volunteer:

- Straightening the magazine area (a consistently trashed part of the teen room)
- Cleaning computer monitors, keyboards, and mice
- Checking DVDs, CDs, and video games for missing disks and running an inventory of missing and broken items that need to be replaced
- Organizing craft supplies
- Entering calendar events into your program schedule
- Creating basic flyers or pamphlets for events
- Tagging materials in the catalog
- Calling teens who have registered for programs to remind them of times and dates
- Editing videos and podcasts
- Posting signs around town
- Making book displays

It would be great if a lot of these tasks could be performed by teens, but some of them could also be good jobs for adults. Do be aware of the creepiness factor of adults hanging out in teen rooms alone—it's probably a good idea to get all of your adult volunteers an ID badge or something else that identifies them as library staff. And if you expect your volunteers to work directly with teens, it's a good idea to make sure that they *like* teens!

Community Partners

There are many reasons to reach out to others in the community. Local businesses can provide financial support, and other nonprofits can share the expense of programs or services. As you spend more time in your library, you will start to learn who in the community is an active youth leader. This could be people in the schools, religious institutions, family centers, or counseling groups. It could be anyone at all. Be open to meeting with others in your community who work with teens, because you will find them an excellent resource for ideas. I will discuss community partners frequently throughout this book, both in terms of outreach, programming, and funding.

Teen Involvement

This is your bread and butter, the theme of all successful teen library programs. Teens themselves are there to help you. If you have formed relationships with any teens, then chances are they have a sense of pride in the library and the teen program. If you have already been giving them a chance to get involved, then you are ready to ask for help. Teens can do all of the tasks listed in the sample volunteering activity list, but they can do so much more.

Publicity. Your number one way of getting teens into the library: word of mouth. If a teen tells a friend that the library is fun, that goes a thousand times farther than you telling a teen the library is fun. Who are you? Just some adult! But teens have credibility with their peers. Recruit them to promote certain events just by word of mouth, or ask them to set up a table in the high school cafeteria (make sure they check with someone at the school first). I would venture that even signs handmade by teens have more credibility than fancy signs made by library staff. An uneven sign with bubble letters and smiley faces screams, "A teen made this!" which equates to, "A teen approves of this!"

Programming support. Teens can have amazing event planning skills. They also know what their peers would want at an event. They can help you set up for events, moving furniture and decorating, or baking snacks, or picking out the music playlists. While I wouldn't feel comfortable asking teens to do this, I have had some teens volunteer to pick up snacks and other supplies with a parent and be reimbursed later. Teens might also enjoy emceeing an event or playing some other role, like handing out programs, staffing refreshment tables, or filming the event.

Media. And speaking of filming, if you can find teens with good audio-visual skills, take advantage. Teens can edit event footage and podcasts, design intros and credits for media, or even compose music to go along with a video tutorial.

Book lists and other collection tools. Ask teens to create bibliographies for summer reading or other events. Make it a collaborative task or have individuals build their own lists, either to be published on your website or printed out and left in the teen area. Or, teens could make bookmarks to tuck into their favorite titles, or put "recommended reads" signs on shelves in the way that bookstores do. Teens can also create their own book displays. You can even ask them to make the signs to go along with it.

2

◇ ◇ ◇

SETTING UP THE TEEN SPACE

If you really are building a teen program from the ground up, then you get to decide what your teen space is going to look like. When I renovated my school library and added a reading nook, I took two of the teen advisory group girls with me to Target and told them to pick out décor (with their parents' permission, of course). If that's not possible or you don't feel comfortable transporting teens, you can always gather around a computer or a catalog to get their thoughts. IKEA is another great source for cheap seating, throw rugs, and wall decoration. It won't last, but it's so cheap that you can replace it when you need to. Another natural source for décor is teen art—solicit your regulars or ask them if they know any artists, or get in touch with the high school art teachers.

I was lucky when I developed the teen space at Darien Library: we had the resources to buy new computers, new furniture, and a flat-panel television. I opted for four iMacs and two PCs, the latter by request because they're better for gaming. The room had six armchairs, most of them with wheels to encourage space rearrangement. The best part of the space was that it was glassed in and the teens could draw on the windows. It would be easy to replicate this with butcher paper and markers—just tear the paper down and put up more when you're ready to have a blank slate. I made writing on the glass a privilege of the teen advisory board members.

The goals of the teen space should be:

Comfort. Soft furniture, floor pillows, throw rugs—all of these things encourage lounging and a feeling of relaxation. You want teens to feel at home in the space, and not like they're going to get in trouble for putting their elbows on the table. Gaming chairs can be perfect providing you have a space that you can set up as a separate gaming area. Beanbag chairs are super comfy but break down easily if you don't spend a lot of money on them. I recommend armchairs—couches can invite shenanigans—and floor pillows as the ideal combination. Teens also seem to love ergonomic computer chairs, and often chose them for gaming over the upholstered furniture at Darien Library. If there is any way you can make the room soundproof, do it. It's probably expensive and a pain in the butt, but the peace of mind for you, your adult patrons, and the teens will be worth it if you can afford it, especially if the teen area abuts a heavily used or typically quiet area used by adults.

Flexibility. Get furniture that can be moved whenever possible. The space is theirs to rearrange as they need to. Study groups should be able to pull all of the chairs into a big circle and teens reading on their own should be able to carve out a cozy corner for themselves. Ottomans are easy to move, and many library-furniture manufacturers make armchairs with wheels. Some tables will be locked into place by wires for computers and the like, but small, moveable tables can be used for homework surfaces or snacks. Some teen librarians use portable screens to create different spaces within the larger space, which is awesome if you have the room. Modular furniture, the kind that can be found at Target or IKEA, isn't super sturdy but works well for displays that can be moved and changed frequently. Another form of flexibility: if you allow food in the teen area (which you should), put in carpet squares. Stained carpet can be easily replaced this way, more cheaply than replacing the whole carpet.

Safety. Teens should always feel safe in the teen space. This means no areas that are hidden from view; no corners where anyone can be, well, cornered; and no furniture that invites some teens to make others feel uncomfortable (i.e., don't make it easy for teens to make out in front of each other). Additionally, you should make sure that the furniture can't be used for harm or that no one would split their head open if they fell on something. Sharp corners and hard surfaces aren't the best idea. If you can have a staff space in the teen area, this is the best way to ensure that everyone who's using the space is being respectful of one another and that no one is putting anyone else in harm's way.

DISPLAY FURNITURE

Teen areas tend to be small. For that reason, you may need to be creative with your display space. At the very least, you can face out books at the ends of shelves, but beyond that, it is a good idea to carve out some kind of space for display. This can be a table, wall-mounted shelves, spinners, or a whole section of stacks devoted just to face-out books. If you can spend some money on new furniture, it's a great idea to get the teens involved. Grab as many catalogs as you can, and invite the Teen Advisory Board to page through them and pick out things that they like. Depending on your space and your budget, you can peruse the following library vendors:

- Demco's teen section—http://www.demco.com/goto?teenspaces— includes a lot of display furniture. (Definitely spend some time looking at their other products if you can, as there's a lot of cool signage, décor, and seating for sale...for a pretty big price tag, though.)
- Gaylord's display furniture (http://www.gaylord.com/listing. asp?H=4) is for all ages, though some is more teen-appropriate than others. For example, check out these revolving graphic novel displays: http://www.gaylord.com/adblock.asp?abid=12872.
- School Outfitters' display stand page (https://www.schoolout fitters.com/catalog/default/cPath/CAT6_CAT56) contains furnishings from different vendors at a wide range of prices.
- Highsmith caters mostly to schools and children's libraries, which means it sells tons of teen-appropriate display furniture: http://www.highsmith.com/displays-20598912/. Some of it, though, is a bit too juvenile-looking for a teen space.
- Finally, Brodart (http://www.brodartfurniture.com/products/shelving-display/index.asp) offers numerous iterations of display shelving and stand-alone furniture.
- For cheaper—and probably less durable—furniture, try the retail stores. A shelf like the one shown at the IKEA website below can be a great way to put books and teen artwork on display, though it looks like it's not terribly sturdy and might need to be placed in a low-traffic area: http://www.ikea.com/us/en/catalog/products/90114752.

RULES FOR THE TEEN SPACE

I hate the idea of rules. Ultimately, the behavior policies of the rest of the library should apply to the teen space, too—nothing more, nothing less. That said, it might be wise to develop a de facto set of behavior guidelines that you can ask teens to abide by. It's been recommended to me that these be posted prominently in a teen space, but I disagree because of the message it sends. Posted rules can give teens the impression that there is an expectation that they will misbehave, and that the staff is more concerned with watching for and punishing bad behavior than allowing teens to be themselves and enjoy the library. As an adult, I feel uncomfortable in spaces with lots of posted "don't" rules, because it suggests a certain strictness that is unappealing. Teens likely feel the same way—perhaps even more so, since they spend much of their day being eyed by authority figures.

Rules or regulations or whatever you wish to call them should really all center around respect. Respect the space, the staff, and your peers. This means no jumping on the furniture, no throwing things, no leaving chewed gum anywhere, no screaming at the top of your lungs. Don't watch anything on the computer that might make someone else feel uncomfortable or that is illegal for underage children to view. Share the resources. Don't damage property or hog the video games. Be fair. It may seem that this is all common sense—because it is. Make sure you're enforcing these rules consistently because teens are amazing at picking up on how adults play favorites or single out one individual or group more than others.

Some things are unacceptable in a space, and, I believe, should result in some kind of action. This action might be asking a teen to leave for the day, or it might mean blocking them from the library for a period of time, or calling parents, or even calling the police in some cases. Consult your library's policies about such things and ask the person who would best know about disciplinary action. Examples of what would be unacceptable: theft, violence, bullying, fighting, vandalism, harassment.

Another consideration is that teens who break minor rules repeatedly must have a consequence. So even if all they're doing is playing their music at unreasonable levels, if you have to ask them twice to turn it down, the second time should be a warning and the third should be a consequence— like asking them to leave. This can be tricky with pre-drivers, and I do think you must be lenient with teens who don't have a ride, as well as avoid sending troublemakers to other areas of the library to be dealt with by another librarian. In these cases, have them sit in an area that you can keep your eye on but away from the teen area. Ask the teen to call her parent or guardian to pick them up. Make sure that teens in this situation know that they are welcome to come back the following day but that you expect them to be more respectful of the space and the people using it. Speak to your colleagues and manager about the incident (some libraries require incident reports) and make sure that everyone is on the same page with the message the teen is receiving.

The point is not to punish teens or make them feel guilty or uncomfortable, but to ensure the enjoyment of the library by others. And I can't stress enough how teens using the library must feel safe. I practice zero tolerance for racial or sexual slurs, bullying, or even teasing based on appearance, gender, sexuality, race, or any other characteristic. If nothing else, the library is a place where people of all backgrounds are treated equally and with respect, and this applies to teens, too.

Filtering

To filter or not to filter—it may not be up to you. Filtering is the practice of using computer programs to block access to certain content online. This content might include sexually explicit, violent, or drug-related content. There are several products available and all are customizable given that you have someone on staff who is comfortable administering the software. Many schools use filtering software, as do many children's rooms. Some schools and libraries choose to filter because they cannot receive certain governmental funding without it. Your library might have a policy already in place. Or an overseeing body—such as the town or the overarching library organization (if you are in a branch)—may make the policy. If you are in the position to have influence over your filtering policy for teen computers—if such a thing exists in your library—then here are the arguments to be made on either side:

Pro Filtering

- If you cannot monitor teen computers well, filtering might help cut down on the number of inappropriate sites visited by teens. This can help make other teens feel comfortable in the space and reduce the amount of illegal computer use, which might occur if you do not have a desk in the room or if some computer screens face away from you.
- Parents may be more comfortable with filtered computers, if they are paying attention to such things.

- If children (under 12) are not restricted from the teen space, you may want to be especially careful about the kinds of websites that are viewable in the room.

Anti Filtering

- Many of the reasons not to filter are philosophical rather than practical, though there are a few reasons why filtering is not practical. For one, filtering does not work as well as we might like. To read more about the failings of filters, read "Just Give It to Me Straight: The Case against Filtering the Internet" at http://faculty.ed.uiuc.edu/burbules/papers/straight.html. The article explains that filters, as computer programs, often make errors in the information they block. The authors cite a 1998 report by the Censorware Project Organization, which makes reference to various legitimate sites blocked by filtering software:
  - Sites blocked for violence included: "an e-zine (electronic magazine) about 'modern Marxism,' the Declaration of Independence, [and] the complete texts of famous works including: *Moby Dick,* the Book of Mormon, [and] the Koran."
  - Sites blocked for sexuality included: "The official *Baywatch* television show website, www.Birthcontrol.com, dozens of news sites that contained any mention of the Starr Report on President Bill Clinton and Monica Lewinsky, and www.mormon.com."

In other words, filtering often filters out acceptable sites.

- Filtering could be considered censorship. Is it the job of the library to decide what sites are appropriate or not for teens—or any patron, for that matter? Or should that be a decision for teens and their parents? You might liken filtering to keeping books behind locked doors. Librarians should think very carefully about limiting access to information of any kind.
- If you have a real presence in the teen area, you will be able to monitor teens' Internet use in a noninvasive way and take opportunities to teach teens about online safety. You can also make teens aware of appropriate Internet use through classes, signs, information on your website, and so on. This is a constructive way to keep teens and children safe online.

No matter what you decide to do, there are a few sites you should be aware of. This list is not meant to be a scare tactic or to blow anything out of proportion, but there are certain sites that you may not feel comfortable having teens visit while in the library:

- Chatroulette (www.chatroulette.com). Much has been written about this site in recent months. It is purportedly limited to those 16 and older, but there is no restriction to who may use the site. On Chatroulette, users have random video chats with strangers from all over the world. As you can imagine, some of these video chats are more appropriate than others. By searching for the name of the site online you will be able to find many articles that address its dangers—and while I do not really think they are dangers per se, I am uncomfortable with teens using the site because of the potential for teens to be exposed to extremely inappropriate live interactions with strangers. In addition, many of the teens I have observed frequenting the site are far younger than 16.
- Formspring (formspring.me). Another site that's been getting a lot of negative buzz, this time for being a venue for cyberbullying. Users post questions for other users that go to their e-mail accounts, and the answers are posted publicly on the user's page. While the site is certainly used by many for innocuous purposes, it has become a tool for teens to publicly denegrate each other, by posing questions such as "why are you such a slut?" And while adults might not understand why, teens are actually *responding* to these questions, lending a certain credibility to the bully. Danah Boyd wrote an eye-opening article, "Harassment by Q&A," about the site, which can be read here: http://dmlcentral.net/blog/danah-boyd/harassment-qa-initial-thoughts-formspringme.

Cyberbullying

I personally find this to be a much more important issue than fears about teens stumbling upon inappropriate information online. Cyberbullying has become a volatile and emotional issue over the past year or two. Teens have fallen victim to cyberbullying at its most extreme—suicides have been all over the news. I think that it is the job of the teen librarian to do whatever he or she can to protect teens from this behavior. Cyberbullying is bullying, period. Bullying is defined as behavior that is aggressive and creates an imbalance of power. It can be physical or verbal and usually takes place over an extended period of time. Cyberbullying can include cruel text messages, posting vulgar things on someone's social networking profile, revealing private information online, or spreading false information about someone online. Teens do not always tell adults—or anyone, for that matter—when they are being cyberbullied; in a 2006 survey, 35 percent of teens who had been cyberbullied said that they told their parents, and only 9 percent had told a teacher.[1] The number one thing that can be done to prevent cyberbullying is for parents to be involved and aware of their children's online activities, but this is not always enough, and it's not always happening. Your role as a librarian and educator is to make the library a safe place. Here's how you can do that:

- Discuss cyberbullying with teens. Make sure they understand what constitutes cyberbullying.
- Do not allow this behavior, ever, in the library. If you see teens cyberbullying another teen—or anyone—treat the issue like you would treat any other behavior issue in the library. Usually this means getting their names and warning them or banning them for a certain amount of time. Make sure that your administrators consider cyberbullying to be included in the library's behavior policy.
- Ask permission before you post teens' images and work on the library website. The last thing you want is for these things to be used to bully. This includes photos, videos, writing, art, and so on. If you can, get parents' permission, too. This may be required by your library as it is.
- Keep in touch with the schools about this issue. If you are witness to a cyberbullying incident, let the school guidance counselor know. See if you can collaborate on educational programs for teens. Ask the guidance counselors how they handle these issues. It's important to establish a relationship about this matter; it helps keep track of repeat offenders and also makes it easier if an incident does take place in the library.
- Educate teens whenever you can. There is a lot of information to be found online, including logos, PSAs, printables like pamphlets and bookmarks, and more. Try the following sites:
  - National Crime Prevention Council's Cyberbullying page—http://www.ncpc.org/topics/cyberbullying
  - Stop Cyberbullying—http://www.stopcyberbullying.org/index2.html
  - Center for Safe & Responsible Internet Use (CSRIU)—http://csriu.org/
  - Connect Safely—http://www.connectsafely.org/ (not just about cyberbullying, but lots of online safety issues)

- Cyberbully 411—http://www.cyberbully411.com/ (for teens)
- Wired Safety—http://wiredsafety.org/
- Text Ed—http://www.lg.com/us/mobile-phones/text-education/homeroom.jsp
- A Thin Line—http://www.athinline.org/ (for teens)
- For more resources, including many for educators, visit Ypulse's excellent collection at http://www.ypulse.com/totally-wired-resources

The key to setting up your teen space is to be flexible, to ask for teen input, and to keep your administration in the loop. We all have an idea of our perfect teen space; this isn't always possible. But even if you can't get everything you want, there are still ways of providing teens with a safe, fun environment in the library, no matter the size of the space. As long as you are keeping teens' comfort and safety in mind, you're doing your job.

NOTE

1. J. Wolak, K. Mitchell, and D. Finkelhor, "Online Victimization of Youth: Five Years Later," *National Center for Missing & Exploited Children Bulletin,* 2006.

3

◇ ◇ ◇

COLLECTION

While it's important to know your community when you start to build a collection, there are also a few basic guidelines that can help you as you begin to buy. I'll outline a smaller, core collection for librarians with smaller budgets, and then suggest ways to expand your collection if you have a little more to spend. Before you do any purchasing, though, you must read over your library's collection development policy, or, if there isn't one, speak to your director about how collection decisions are made in your library.

THE COLLECTION DEVELOPMENT POLICY

This section will specifically address policies for young adult collections. If your library has not focused on young adult collections in the past, there may not already be a section on teen materials in the existing collection development policy. There is no need to reinvent the wheel. In addition, you should see what you can find on other libraries' websites. Many post their collection development policies for the public to access. Most sections on teen materials are from one to three paragraphs long and include:

- Categories of materials added to the collection (high-interest young adult fiction, homework support, award-winners, materials found on collection development lists)

- The age range served by the collection; this can vary by library
- Criteria used to collect materials: the age of the characters, the theme, the subject matter, and so forth.

Here's one example of a young adult collection policy, as included in the Pasadena Public Library's Collection Development policy:

Young Adult Collection

A limited young adult collection has been established at Central and some of the branches to satisfy the library needs of patrons from the approximate age of 13 to 18 years. It is a transitional collection for the reader moving from the children's collection to the adult collection. The type of materials selected differs significantly from the junior high level because of the social, emotional, and intellectual maturity required to read them. As this is primarily a browsing collection, fiction and paperbacks are emphasized with a selection of topical nonfiction and hardback books. While materials of overall "good literary quality" are included in this collection, popular titles and themes of contemporary interest to the target age groups are stressed.

Look online for more examples, either in your region or at libraries with successful teen programs. In addition to using other libraries' policies as a guide, writing a collection development policy is an exercise that should be undertaken by you and any involved staff. In a way, this mimics the process of writing a mission statement. As I mentioned before, if your library already has a collection development policy, you will only be undertaking the writing of a new section of that existing policy, which means that you may be able to leave some sections out (an introduction to the entire policy, for example). Here are some resources to help you along:

- The Arizona State Library has a comprehensive write-up on collection development policies—what they are, why they're important, and what the major elements are: http://www.lib.az.us/cdt/colldev.aspx.
- The Idaho Commission for Libraries offers an exercise for librarians undergoing the collection development writing process: http://www.lili.org/forlibs/ce/able/course1/19writing.htm.
- Scarecrow Press's *Library Collection Development Policies: Academic, Public, and Special Libraries*, written by Frank Hoffman in 2004, is a comprehensive overview of writing a policy from start to finish.

A collection development policy is crucial for several reasons. For a start, it provides a framework for your acquisitions, and it is a resource if you are unsure about whether or not to purchase an item. An emphasis on popular, high-interest materials purchased for pleasure reading means that you are able to support the purchase of a broad range of materials with your policy. When it comes to purchasing books, magazines, and other materials for teens, you will not only be purchasing the highest quality materials but also those that will be popular and attractive to teens. This means that you'll be purchasing series books and other titles that are not reviewed in the trade journals, as well as magazines that sometimes feature mature content, like *Rolling Stone* and *TransWorld Skateboarding*. It also means that you'll be purchasing books that are not necessarily considered highbrow. If you go by your policy, you may feel more comfortable purchasing these high-interest materials. Additionally, if an item in your collection is ever questioned or challenged, you will be able to point to your collection development policy as a justification for why you purchased that particular item. A well-written collection development policy is not a safeguard against challenges to collections; nor is it a failsafe defense against them. But it is a document, approved by your director and board, that you can refer to in these situations. It helps you feel less alone.

EVALUATING WHAT YOU ALREADY HAVE

It may not take you long to figure out what subjects your teens are interested in, but it's important to be aware of niche interests. Just because your *Gossip Girl, Clique,* and *A-List* series books fly off the shelf doesn't mean that you don't have readers who want brainy fantasy novels or literary fiction. Public librarians should talk to the local school librarians and English teachers to see what the teens are already reading for pleasure. If you've connected with any area teens online, see what they list as their favorite books in their profiles. And ask all the teens you see. Don't just ask what books they like to read; ask what their favorite television shows are, which magazines they like best, and what bands they listen to. All of these things will help give you a complete picture of the diverse interests of the teens in your community.

Chances are, there are already young adult titles in your library. Review the upper levels of the children's room collection, as well as adult titles that appeal to teens. If your library is automated, you can check the circulation statistics on popular authors. Some suggestions:

Adult fiction authors (some of these authors also publish young adult titles)

Douglas Adams

Sherman Alexie

Orson Scott Card

Sandra Cisneros

Neil Gaiman

Mark Haddon

Nick Hornby

Stephen King

Megan McCafferty (whose books may already be shelved in a teen section)

Blake Nelson

Jodi Picoult

Alice Sebold

David Sedaris

Kurt Vonnegut

Children's fiction books

Tangerine by Edward Bloor

Pieces of Georgia by Jen Bryant

The Dark is Rising series by Susan Cooper

The House of the Scorpion by Nancy Farmer

The Graveyard Book by Neil Gaiman

Shug by Jenny Han

The *Skulduggery Pleasant* series by Derek Landy

Jeremy Fink and the Meaning of Life by Wendy Mass

Kiki Strike: Inside the Shadow City by Kristen Miller

Hatchet by Gary Paulson

The Wee Free Men by Terry Pratchett

The Wednesday Wars by Gary Schmidt

The *Homecoming* series by Cynthia Voigt

The children's library no doubt contains many books that can be moved into your new teen space or at least duplicated. If the head of children's services allows it, take a few days to go through the fiction collection and pull out the titles that you think might work in a teen collection. I caution you to not allow your collection to go too young; a middle-grade collection will result in middle-grade users. That said, you need to be aware of how teens in your community read. If children and teens read up, then many books you might consider "teen" will stay in—or be duplicated in—the children's collection; if they read down, then you may have more of those younger titles in the teen collection. But content is important. Books at a lower reading level cannot also be at a lower content level, because teens don't want to read about children's issues or about characters that are still in elementary school. If you are serving a population of teens who read down, then you will need to invest in what are called "high/low" books—high interest, low reading level. More on that later.

Once you have pulled together as many books as possible that are already in the library, analyze what you've got. If your Integrated Library System (ILS) has a collection analysis tool, you're in luck. These tools usually require you to download all of your records in a specific format and then run that file through a program that sorts and analyzes the data. The data is then presented to you in various ways. You may be able to determine the average age of your collection, or figure out how many books in the collection were published after a certain date. Tools like this are great for weeding, either now or later on. Another helpful way to sort data is by circulation statistics. See which books have circulated the most and keep or replace them with new copies. Those that have circulated the least can be withdrawn or put on display to beef up their stats. You will learn a lot about how your current group of teen patrons reads from these numbers—but they don't mean everything because, of course, they only represent the teens that were checking out books from the children's collection.

If you can figure out how your collection is broken down by genre, you will be in an excellent position to determine which genres need to be fleshed out. Generally speaking, the main genres in teen fiction are realistic fiction, historical fiction, fantasy, science fiction, and paranormal or horror. Others to consider: adventure, mystery, romance (and chick lit), urban/street lit, humor. If you like, you can also separate nonfiction out into genres, like "all about me," sports, paranormal, biography and memoir, arts and crafts, and so on. And you will also have to decide whether you'd like to interfile your graphic novels or if you would prefer to contain all of your graphic novels in one section. How do you think teens would best find information?

THE CORE COLLECTION

There are some excellent books that address the idea of the core collection. These books tend to contain lists of books separated out by genre (or some other category) and the booklists are annotated. Some are more current than others, which you should be aware of. They are:

Barr, Catherine, and John T. Gillespie. *Best Books for High School Readers, Grades 9–12.* Santa Barbara: Libraries Unlimited, 2009.

Barr, Catherine, and John T. Gillespie. *Best Books for Middle School and Junior High Readers, Grades 6–9.* Santa Barbara: Libraries Unlimited, 2009.

Booth, Heather. *Serving Teens through Readers' Advisory.* Chicago: ALA, 2007.

Cart, Michael. *Young Adult Literature: From Romance to Realism.* Chicago: ALA, 2010.

Fraser, Elizabeth. *Reality Rules! A Guide to Teen Nonfiction Reading Interests.* Westport, CT: Libraries Unlimited, 2008.

Herald, Diana Tixier. *Teen Genreflecting: A Guide to Reading Interests.* Santa Barbara: Libraries Unlimited, 2010.

Holley, Pam Spencer. *Quick and Popular Reads for Teens.* Chicago: ALA, 2009.

Jones, Patrick, Patricia Taylor, and Kristen Edwards. *A Core Collection for Young Adults.* New York: Neal-Schuman, 2003.

Koelling, Holly. *Best Books for Young Adults.* Chicago: ALA, 2009.

Lesesne, Teri. *Making the Match: The Right Book for the Right Reader at the Right Time,* Grades 4–12. Portland, ME: Stenhouse, 2003.

Nilsen, Alleen, and Kenneth L. Donelson. *Literature for Today's Young Adults.* Boston: Allyn & Bacon, 2008.

Silvey, Anita. *500 Great Books for Teens.* New York: Houghton Mifflin Harcourt, 2006.

Thomas, Rebecca L., and Catherine Barr. *Popular Series Fiction for Middle School and Teen Readers.* Westport, CT: Libraries Unlimited, 2008.

Zbaracki, Matthew D. *Best Books for Boys.* Westport, CT: Libraries Unlimited, 2008.

Ask your children's librarians if they already own any of these. If not, try to pick up one or two. While books like this lack the immediacy of websites—and cannot be updated nearly as frequently—they are easy to use and refer back to.

Another great place to start is with reader's advisory databases, which may be available through your library or the school library. These databases feature excellent collection development tools, such as genre and recommended reading lists; suggestions based on the books one has read; and collections of full-text reviews for each title. Depending on the database, users can search for books by topic, genre, setting, character, location, or timeframe. Some databases may allow users to create their own custom lists of titles. Others include teaching and book group guides and annotated lists. All of these tools can be extremely useful to you. Some of the best known RA databases are:

- Fiction Connection (Bowker)
- NoveList
- Reader's Advisor Online
- Books and Authors (Gale)

DIGGING DEEPER

The next section of this chapter discusses selection tools, and you will also find information on lists published by various organizations. The following resources are intended to help you mostly with building large portions of the collection, as opposed to ongoing collection development.

When it comes time to dig a little deeper, beyond the core collection but still with an eye toward building a collection foundation, you will need to have a sense of which genres are most popular with teens in your community. Once you get a feeling for this, you can start developing certain collections more heavily. Try these titles for inspiration:

Bodart, Joni Richards. *Radical Reads 2: Working with the Newest Edgy Titles for Teens.* Lanham, MD: Scarecrow, 2010. [*Note: Radical Reads 1* was published in 2002.]

Fichtelburg, Susan. *Encountering Enchantment: A Guide to Speculative Fiction for Teens.* Westport, CT: Libraries Unlimited, 2006.

Goldsmith, Francisca. *The Reader's Advisory Guide to Graphic Novels.* Chicago: ALA, 2010. [*Note:* not just for teen readers.]

Honig, Megan. *Urban Grit: A Guide to Street Lit.* Santa Barbara: Libraries Unlimited, 2011. [*Note:* not just for teen readers.]

Pawuk, Mike. *Graphic Novels: A Genre Guide to Comics, Manga, and More.* Westport. CT: Libraries Unlimited, 2006. [*Note:* titles for teens are tagged]

Rabey, Melissa: *Historical Fiction for Teens: A Genre Guide.* Santa Barbara: Libraries Unlimited, 2010.

Schall, Lucy. *Genre Talks for Teens: Booktalks and More for Every Teen Reading Interest.* Santa Barbara: Libraries Unlimited, 2009.

Wadham, Rachel. *This Is My Life: A Guide to Realistic Fiction for Teens.* Santa Barbara: Libraries Unlimited, 2010.

Additionally, you will find seemingly limitless numbers of genre booklists online. Again, check RA databases for genre lists. Among the free online resources, here are a few of those I like. In the case when a site has unique categories, I have listed some of my favorites underneath:

- Library Booklists—a compilation of library booklists: http://library booklists.org
- ATN Reading Lists—a wiki featuring librarians' booklists: http:// atn-reading-lists.wikispaces.com/Genre
  - "Clean" Romance
  - Hip Hop Literature
  - Southern Fiction
  - Teen Authors
- Reading Rants—not your ordinary booklists: http://www.readin grants.org/
  - Boy Meets Book
  - Short Cuts
  - Tearjerkers
  - Gods and Monsters
- The Mid-Continent Public Library's Recommended Teen Reading Lists: http://www.mymcpl.org/teens/recommended-books-movies-music-teens
  - I'm with the Band
  - Help Me Accept Myself
  - But I Hate To Read
  - From Across the Sea
  - I Have Issues

NEW MEDIA

Teen collections aren't just about books, and you will need to start off with some nonprint materials in the space in order to fully serve the teens using the collection. This might mean different things for different libraries, but the main areas of nonprint collection are video games, movies, music, and audiobooks. A good book for an overview of nonprint materials is C. Allen Nichols's *Thinking Outside the Book: Alternatives for Today's Teen Library Collections* (Westport, CT: Libraries Unlimited, 2004).

Games

When it comes time to create your video game collection, you will need to think carefully about the criteria by which games will be purchased.

Because video games are often a tricky collection item, it's worth spending a little time on these acquisition guidelines. Besides thinking about basic things like format and genre, make sure you understand video game ratings and have a sense of which ratings are appropriate for a teen audience—and, more specifically, an audience of teen library users. In other words, games that may be all right in the home may not be all right in the library.

- E (Everyone): contains content appropriate for ages six and older. Limited or no violence. The equivalent of a G rating for a movie. Examples: *NFL Head Coach, Gran Turismo 4, Dance Dance Revolution Mario Mix*.
- E-10 (Everyone 10+): contains content unsuitable for children under 10. May contain mild violence, including what's called "cartoon violence" or "fantasy violence." In other words, the violence is not realistic. The equivalent of a PG rating for a movie. Examples: Kung Fu Panda, Shaun White Snowboarding, Sonic Unleashed.
- T (Teen): contains content unsuitable for children under 13. May contain violence, suggestive themes, crude humor, and strong language. Violence might be more realistic in nature—red blood versus no blood at all, for example. The equivalent of a PG-13 rating for a movie. Examples: *Super Smash Brothers Brawl, Tomb Raider Legend, Tony Hawk's American Wasteland*.
- M (Mature): contains content unsuitable for children under 17 years old. Violence can be more intense, might contain sexual content, nudity, strong language, blood and gore. An R-rated game. Examples: *Hitman 2: Silent Assassin, Resident Evil: Outbreak, Grand Theft Auto, Halo 3*.

You might think about looking at your library's policy for lending movies. Can children or teens check out R-rated films, or do they need a parent's permission? Must they be 13 to check out PG-13 movies? What about CDs with parental advisory warnings? If none of these things provide you with any guidance, I recommend limiting the games available to teens to those rated T. I say this because if these games are played in the library, then M-rated games may make some teens uncomfortable. Additionally, R-rated movies would not typically be shelved in the teen area for teens as young as 12 to check out; the same should hold true for games. This is just my opinion, though, and you should think carefully about how you want to approach this issue.

Once you have decided what kind of games you will be purchasing—based on rating, genre, age level, and the like—then the following websites are good places to look for recommendations. (But don't forget to ask the teens!)

- IGN. http://www.ign.com/. The review section contains easy-to-navigate top reviewed and recently reviewed games, and you may also search for the titles of specific games. Pay attention to both of these lists, as teens love both popular, high-quality games and new games. IGN also has an amazing section of game walk-throughs, cheats, and hints.
- Gamespot. http://www.gamespot.com/. Like IGN, Gamespot's review section allows you to search for specific titles and also offers the ability to limit by platform and genre. The new releases section highlights upcoming and new games.
- Gametrailers. http://www.gametrailers.com/. Similar to the other sites, but I like it because game trailers can be fun to watch and give you great insight into the look and feel of certain games.
- *Wired.* http://www.wired.com/reviews/productlisting/gaming_gear. The tech mag has a useful section on gaming gear only, with at-a-glance ratings. Additionally, *Wired*'s *Gamelife* blog (http://www.wired.com/gamelife/) provides news on new and exciting games, the gaming industry, and roundups of information about gaming, including its educational benefits, movie tie-ins, new technology, and so on.
- *Joystiq.* http://www.joystiq.com/. This blog provides news about the gaming industry and often posts trailers of note, links to online games, and reviews.

Movies

It's almost a certainty that your library already circulates DVDs (and maybe even VHS tapes!). DVDs make up much of public libraries' circulation. Who is in charge of purchasing these materials? Is there a separate children's collection? Just as you did with books, see if there are duplicates that can be moved into the teen area. Beyond that, approach movie purchasing in the same way that you approach acquiring any other materials: think about your audience. Try to find a balance of quality and interest. There are lots of movies that are perfect for a teen audience, though unlike books and even games, many of these movies are not marketed specifically to teens. So it may take a bit more work on your part to get this collection together. Here are a few books that could help:

Barr, Catherine. *Best New Media, K–12: A Guide to Movies, Subscription Web Sites, and Educational Software and Games.* Westport, CT: Libraries Unlimited, 2008. [*Note:* this book includes more than just movies.]

Halsall, Jane, Edminster, R. William, and C. Allen Nichols. *Visual Media for Teens: Creating and Using a Teen-Centered Film Collection.* Santa Barbara, CA: Libraries Unlimited, 2009.

Movies that appeal to teens usually feature characters who are around the same age as they are—in high school or college. There is also a slew of movies with adult characters that teens love. Popular films range from cult classics to the new classics to the biggest blockbusters around. I'll list some samples below and then also point you toward some others' lists of suggested films for teens.

Suggested films

10 Things I Hate About You

17 Again

Avatar

Percy Jackson & The Olympians: The Lightning Thief

The *American Pie* franchise: the original three are *American Pie*, *American Pie 2*, and *American Wedding* (there are others in the franchise, but they were direct to DVD).

The *Austin Powers* franchise: *International Man of Mystery*, *The Spy who Shagged Me*, and *Goldmember*

Bring It On

All the *Marvel* movies: *Fantastic 4*, *Spider-Man*, the *X-Men* series

Dear John

The *Harry Potter* franchise:

Harry Potter and the Sorcerer's Stone

Harry Potter and the Chamber of Secrets

Harry Potter and the Prisoner of Azkaban

Harry Potter and the Goblet of Fire

Harry Potter and the Order of the Phoenix

Harry Potter and the Half-Blood Prince

Harry Potter and the Deathly Hallows parts 1 and 2 (part 2 to be released July 2011)

The *High School Musical* franchise:

   High School Musical

   High School Musical 2

   High School Musical 3: Senior Year

   High School Musical 4: East Meets West

Juno

Legally Blonde

The Lord of the Rings trilogy

Mean Girls

Napoleon Dynamite

The *National Lampoon* franchise

Nick and Norah's Infinite Playlist

The *Transformers* series

The *Twilight* series: *Twilight, New Moon, Eclipse,* and *Breaking Dawn* parts 1 and 2 (to be released in November 2011 and November 2012, respectively)

Any Will Farrell, Chris Farley, Dane Cook, or Adam Sandler movie

Most *Saturday Night Live* spin-off films, for example:

   Wayne's World and Wayne's World 2

   A Night at the Roxbury

   McGruber

Spoof films like *Scary Movie, Not Another Teen Movie, Tropic Thunder,* or *Epic Movie*

   Youth in Revolt

   Zombieland

   The Blind Side

Horror films of all shapes and sizes

Documentaries

   An Inconvenient Truth

   Michael Moore movies (*Bowling for Columbine, Fahrenheit 9/11, Capitalism: A Love Story*)

   Food, Inc.

   This Is It

   Super Size Me

   The Cove

Lists

- YALSA's Fabulous Films for Young Adults was started in 1997, and rather than selecting films by year, creates lists based on themes. Therefore, all of these lists, from 1997, are relevant and useful. http://www.ala.org/ala/mgrps/divs/yalsa/booklistsawards/fabfilms/fabfilms.cfm

- Common Sense Media lists recommended movies for teens at http://www.commonsensemedia.org/movie-lists/ages-15–17. Be aware that CSM exists to advise parents on which materials—books, movies, and the like—are most appropriate for their children, and therefore these selections are created with that criteria in mind. Despite this, it is a useful resource.

- AMC Filmsite's 50 best High School Movies (http://www.filmsite.org/50besthsfilms.html) contains lots of classics that teens will turn up their noses to, but there are some contemporary films on the list that are definitely worth considering.

- The Mid-Continent Public Library has a wonderful resource on its website, Based on the Book, which is a database of all the films that have ever been adapted from books. Using lists like this can be an excellent way to promote books through movies and vice versa. http://www.mcpl.lib.mo.us/readers/movies/

Reviews and movie news

- MTV's *Movies Blog* (http://moviesblog.mtv.com/) is written for a teen and young adult audience, and while it doesn't contain recommended lists, it does call your attention to new and notable films that will certainly be of interest to teens.

- *Entertainment Weekly* (http://www.ew.com/ew/movies/) posts reviews, insider information, box office information, awards predictions, and more.

- *Rolling Stone* (http://www.rollingstone.com/movies) posts reviews, interviews, top-five lists, DVD releases, and movie news.

- *The New York Times*'s movie reviews (http://movies.nytimes.com/pages/movies/index.html) don't just feature high-brow flicks, as one might suspect, but the reviews tend to be long and don't necessarily address whether or not the film would appeal to teens. But they are a delight to read.

- Rotten Tomatoes is a favorite (http://www.rottentomatoes.com/) because it aggregates all of other critical reviews of a film and then assigns the film a rating based on the overall rottenness or freshness of the reviews. These can be fun for teens to read.

Reviews are condensed into a one- or two- sentence highlight, but you can link to the full text from the site.

Music

More than any other category, I think, music is the most intimidating to collect for teens. You might not be listening to the kind of music that teens like, and it is harder to be aware of new and popular music than it is of movies, simply because there is far more music being released than there are movies. Happily, there are a few resources that address the topic, and there are many places to go for reviews. Most of all, ask the teens what they are listening to. Not all teens listen to bubblegum pop, and depending on your geographical area, some musical genres will be more popular than others. If you are friends with teens online, you can view their musical interests in their profiles. You might also set up a suggestion box or binder where teens can recommend CD purchases.

Also consider format. CDs are still best, I think, because they are easy to circulate and can be loaded onto MP3 players and laptops. This does raise copyright issues, of course, but I am not sure that this can be avoided at this time, until all CDs are outfitted with Digital Rights Management that does not allow MP3 files to be loaded onto more than one device. (I don't mean by that statement that I approve of DRM.) If you can legally offer music downloads somehow, do it—and let me know how! I have yet to discover a way to lend music digitally without purchasing an MP3 for someone, which is not an affordable model.

Reviews and Music News

- Not so much a review site, but join YALSA's Teen Music Interest Group by visiting http://lists.ala.org/wws/info/ya-music. The group discusses "recommended practices in collections, programming, and related topics in the field of music and media, including CDs, MP3s, and emerging technologies and services in music media for teens."

- Denver Public Library has an amazing site where teens can write reviews of CDs. Visit it at http://teens.denverlibrary.org/reviews/reviews.cfm?media=Music. This is a fabulous way to get teen input.

- Teen Vogue's Music Blogger, Leigh Belz, writes at http://www.teenvogue.com/industry/blogs/music. Her write-ups likely reflect the interests of many of your teens. She writes mostly about pop, though the music she features tends to be a bit edgier than your standard top-forty fare.

- MTV has several music features, as you might imagine. All of them will be of interest to teen audiences. They are:
  - Buzzworthy. http://buzzworthy.mtv.com/. Upcoming music and music-related news that's getting a lot of attention.
  - Music News. http://www.mtv.com/news/#music/. Simply put, anything related to music...at all.
  - The main music page—http://www.mtv.com/music/—has video playlists and top ten artist lists.
- Teen Music, at http://www.teenmusic.com/, seems to be more for the tween set, featuring young pop stars on its main page more often than not. However, it also features dozens of videos by bands that run the gamut from rap to indie rock.
- Allmusic (http://www.allmusic.com/) is not a site to go to if you don't know what you're looking for, but it is an excellent resource for finding out more about bands and artists, including related music—for example, if you like Weezer, you might like...
- Finally, visit the websites of your local radio stations—many of them publish playlists—stay on top of YouTube's top music videos, and visit the iTunes store to see the top downloads.

ORGANIZING YOUR COLLECTION

At Darien Library, I divided the teen collection up into genre categories. They were:

Realistic fiction

Fantasy

Historical fiction

Graphic novels[1]

Series (books that are part of an open-ended series, not trilogies, etc.)

Science Fiction

Horror

Nonfiction

You may wish to divide up your collection further—mystery, humor, romance, and adventure are all examples of genres that appeal to teens and often show up in teen collections. If you choose not to divide your collection by genre, I recommend using genre stickers to help your users, who tend to look for books that way, find what they're looking for.

There are a few benefits to shelving by genre. Teen readers often are drawn to particular genres or like to read books that are similar to others they enjoyed. A frequent reader's advisory question is: "I just read *The Hunger Games*. What else do you have that is like that?" In those situations, it's great to be able to point teens to the science fiction or adventure section. Shelving by genre also allows teens to help themselves to these books, and empowering the user is always a good thing. Shelving by genre is also a great way for you to see your collection at a glance and figure out which sections need to be weeded, added to, promoted, and so on. In this model, readers may also find materials by using the catalog as long as the call numbers somehow reflect how the item is shelved. The easiest way to do this is to create a prefix that points the user toward a particular section— "YA HIST" for historical fiction, for example, or "YA FANTASY." Along with this, the shelves must be clearly labeled in order to make it very easy to users to find the item they're looking for.

There is one major challenge that emerges when a collection is shelved by genre. Patrons who are looking for a specific author and who do not use the catalog are used to being able to go to the "C" section, for example, to find Meg Cabot books. If Meg Cabot's books are shelved in more than one place, then the patron will not be able to quickly and easily find all of her books. In these cases, you will need to educate teens on how the collection is arranged and how it can be used. I have found that with time, teens have become accustomed to this new method of searching for books. Another challenge is yours, not the teens'—where do you shelve books that cross genres? The *Twilight* books, for example—are they fantasy, horror, or romance? In this case, you have to make the best decision you can, and you might consider shelving these books in more than one section, if you can afford multiple copies.

ONGOING SELECTION TOOLS

Traditional review sources include journals like *School Library Journal, Booklist, Horn Book, Library Journal,* and *Publisher's Weekly.* I also consider booklists, especially those produced by libraries and library organizations, to be traditional. Teen librarians should also pay close attention to the various teen book awards presented every year.

Booklists

YALSA's booklists can be found at http://ala.org/ala/mgrps/divs/yalsa/booklistsawards/booklistsbook.cfm. They include:

- Amazing Audio Books for Young Adults
- Best Fiction for Young Adults (recently changed—was the Best Books for Young Adults)
- Fabulous Films for Young Adults
- Great Graphic Novels for Teens
- Outstanding Books for the College Bound
- Popular Paperbacks for Young Adults [thematic booklists]
- Quick Picks for Reluctant Young Adult Readers
- Teens' Top Ten

Another wonderful list put out every year is New York Public Library's Stuff for the Teen Age, which can be found at http://legacy.www.nypl.org/books/sta2009/.

Mentioned earlier but worth mentioning again is Reading Rants! Out of the Ordinary Teen Booklists, the brainchild of Jen Hubert Swan. These booklists are traditional in a way, because they center around themes, but the themes themselves are funny, cool, and edgy—just like teens themselves. http://www.readingrants.org/

Teen Book Awards

YALSA awards the most honors to teen books. YALSA's major awards and lists are announced in January at the ALA Midwinter conference.

- The Printz Award is the big, big winner in teen lit every year, though critics sometimes say that the picks appeal more to adult librarians than to teen readers. www.ala.org/yalsa/printz/
- The Alex Award is given to teen adult books that appeal to teens. I always think this is a great list, and these books are definitely worth purchasing for a teen collection if you have readers who enjoy literary fiction and/or reading above their grade level. http://www.ala.org/ala/mgrps/divs/yalsa/booklistsawards/alexawards/alexawards.cfm
- The Margaret A. Edwards Award is a prize given to an author for their body of work. http://www.ala.org/ala/mgrps/divs/yalsa/booklistsawards/margaretaedwards/margaretedwards.cfm
- The William C. Morris Award is a librarian favorite and honors a debut teen novel by a first-time author every year. http://www.ala.org/ala/mgrps/divs/yalsa/booklistsawards/morris/morrisaward.cfm

- The Odyssey Award is a joint YALSA/ALSC award that honors the best audiobook of the year for children or young adults—so be aware of the audience for this one. http://www.ala.org/ala/mgrps/divs/yalsa/booklistsawards/odyssey/odyssey.cfm
- The YALSA Award for Excellence in Nonfiction for Young Adults is a new award introduced in 2010. http://www.ala.org/ala/mgrps/divs/yalsa/booklistsawards/nonfiction/nonfiction.cfm

The National Book Award for Young Readers is presented by The National Book Foundation every year. It can honor fiction or nonfiction, and some of those books that win the award or are shortlisted are middle grade, such as 2009's winner, *Claudette Colvin: Twice Toward Justice* by Philip Hoose (http://www.nationalbook.org/nba2009.html). The categories are judged by other authors in that particular genre. The NBF posts footage of its awards ceremony online.

Many states host their own book awards. Search for the name of your state plus the words *teen book award* and you should find what you're looking for. But look at other states' awards, too. Cynthia Leitich Smith lists all of them on her website: http://www.cynthialeitichsmith.com/lit_resources/awards/stateawards.html.

A relatively recent award is the Cybils, the annual children's and young adult literary awards. Aside from the Young Adult Fiction award, there are awards in Young Adult Fantasy & Science Fiction, Graphic Novels, and Young Adult Nonfiction. The winners are annotated and the site also publishes the nominees and the names of those who nominated each title (usually an author or librarian): http://www.cybils.com/.

Amazon.com publishes its Top 100 Editors' Picks every year around the winter holidays and highlights the top 10. These books could be written for any age; in 2009, one young adult book (*Beautiful Creatures*) and one Alex Award winner (*Stitches*) were in the top ten list. Additionally, Amazon publishes its editors' picks for young adult books and the Top 100 Customer Favorites. Amazon introduced its Breakthrough Novel Award in 2008, which has two categories: General Fiction and Young Adult Fiction (the YA Fiction category is judged by established young adult authors).

Similarly, Barnes & Noble has presented the Discover Awards for 17 years; they do not, however, have a young adult category. Barnes & Noble does not seem to focus on young adult books quite as much with its selection tools; its "Barnes & Noble Recommends" section is also only for adult books and teen books are listed in the children's section and do not have their own featured page.

The Boston Globe–*Horn Book* Awards are awarded annually to children's and young adult titles. Two honor books are also selected in each category. Like the National Book Foundation, the *Horn Book* website posts footage of its award ceremonies: http://www.hbook.com/bghb/default.asp.

Not as austere but a whole lot of fun are the Kids' Choice Awards, a televised awards show broadcast on Nickelodeon. While, sadly, the Teen Choice Awards does not have a book category, the Kids' Choice Awards does. In 2009, the nominated titles included *Twilight* and *The Vampire Diaries*, both YA books, though *Diary of a Wimpy Kid*, a middle grade book, won: http://www.nick.com/kids-choice-awards/.

For a comprehensive list of teen book awards, including many not on this list, visit Cynthia Leitich Smith's national awards page at http://www.cynthialeitichsmith.com/lit_resources/awards/nat_awards.html.

Nontraditional review sources include blogs, websites, and trade magazines. Some of my favorites are included in the following list.

> *Blogs* (I recommend adding all of these to a blog reader like Google Reader or Bloglines in order to keep up.)

> *3 Evil Cousins:* http://3evilcousins.blogspot.com/
> *Bookmoot:* http://www.bookmoot.com/
> *Bookshelves of Doom:* http://bookshelvesofdoom.blogs.com/book shelves_of_doom/
> *The Longstockings:* http://thelongstockings.blogspot.com/
> *The YA YA YAs:* http://theyayayas.wordpress.com/
> *Trashionista:* http://www.trashionista.com/
> *Young Adult Books Central:* http://yabookscentral.blogspot.com/
> *Teen Vogue Book Blog:* http://www.teenvogue.com/industry/blogs/entertainment/books/
> *Book Burger:* http://bookburger.typepad.com/
> *Guys Read:* http://www.guysread.com/
> *No Flying, No Tights:* http://www.noflyingnotights.com/index2.html
> *YA Fresh:* http://yafresh.blogspot.com/
> *Pink Me:* http://pinkme.typepad.com/
> *Queer YA:* http://daisyporter.org/queerya/

> *Websites* (Bookseller websites are good places to look, too.)

> YA Lit Book Release Dates: http://www.yalit.com/
> Teens Read Too: http://www.teensreadtoo.com/

Trade magazines (These magazines aren't known for their book reviews, but they publish them often—sometimes in every issue—and will highlight titles that teens are sure to hear about.)

Seventeen
Entertainment Weekly
People
Teen Vogue

KNOWING YOUR READERS AND YOUR COMMUNITY

When I was at Darien Library, I knew that certain genres would never fly with my teens. They tended to like series fiction, sci fi, and realistic fiction. They didn't read much nonfiction. Stories in urban settings didn't go out, and historical fiction only got read when they had an assignment. And the fantasy section, while used heavily by many, was overstuffed, which told me it was too big.

As you spend more time getting to know the teens that use your library, you'll start to discover trends and patterns in the books they borrow and ask about. When you booktalk to hand-sell a title, you'll see their reactions. Although, as a caveat, I have had many teens stare blankly at me as I talk to them about a book, only to have them smile and accept it at the end as though they can't wait to get home to read it. Teens are very good about telling you when a book you're recommending is not interesting to them. They'll make a face and say "do you have anything else?" This is a good opportunity to ask them about what they like to read. The more of these conversations you have, the more you will get a sense of the reading habits of your community.

Teen collections don't exist in a vacuum. The kids' books have to leave off somewhere, and a lot of teens are reading adult books by the time they hit high school (or younger). I kept a very few adult books in the teen collection—Jodi Picoult, for one—but usually left that to the adult fiction buyers. There was also some crossover with the children's room collection, but it's important to communicate with the children's staff about stuff like this so that there isn't a *ton* of duplication, which can get confusing and expensive. Talking to your children's librarians will also give you a sense of whether teens in your community read up or read down. Reading up means that a lot of the books you might have bought really belong in the children's collection; reading down means you might have more duplication, or the children's collection might leave off earlier, which is where you should pick up.

There's something to be said for keeping lower reading level books in the teen room if you think teens are looking for them. Teens who read down will not want to go to the children's room. Additionally, as mentioned previously, there are lots of great books out there that are considered "high/low"—high interest, low reading level. I'll talk a little more about that in the Reluctant Reader section later on.

It would behoove the teen librarian to at least be an observer in the adult collection development process, in order to know what's being bought that could be of interest to teens. If you're able to, make suggestions, not only for high-interest fiction, but also for nonfiction that could be used for homework or research projects. Reference librarians probably know a great deal about the kinds of research projects that come through the library every year. Even if your collection does not include homework materials, be aware.

All this is well and good, but if you're new to your library, you probably have no idea what teens in your community like to read. This is a great chance for you to gather information by speaking with your colleagues, people in your community, and most of all, teens. How? Here are some places to start.

- *Focus groups.* Many librarians have undertaken focus groups as a way to gather information about what teens like to do in the library and what they like to read. If you are running focus groups anyway to find out more information about what teens want to get out of the library, make sure you're including questions about what they like to read.
- *Surveys.* Either leave paper surveys out in the teen area, distribute them through the school English teachers, post polls on your website, or ask teens to vote on a display of books in the teen space.
- *ILS data.* Can you run reports that show you which books have the most holds on them or are checked out most frequently? If so, this information will tell you a lot about what's getting read—or at least, what's circulating (yes, there is a difference).
- *Casual conversations with teens you know.* Ask your Teen Advisory Board members, the kids who come to programs, the teens you chat with in the space. You can't assume that one teen's tastes represent the whole, but all of this information contributes to the big picture.

THE RELUCTANT READER

What defines a reluctant reader? The Young Adult Library Association simply says that a reluctant reader is someone who "for whatever reason, doesn't like to read." There are several reasons why some teens might not like to read. Perhaps reading is difficult for them. Or maybe they find reading boring, they feel they don't have enough time to read, or reading is not valued by those who are important to them—their families, friends, or peers. As a teen librarian, you have the opportunity to put books into the hands of reluctant readers that they might actually want to read. In order to do this, you'll need to educate yourself a little on how reading can be encouraged and discouraged.

What Not to Do

Reading is not the be-all and end-all. We don't trick kids into reading by luring them into the library to play video games and then forcing them to look at books. We don't judge teens who don't like to read. It's not our job to value certain books above others or certain interests above others. Criticism and pressure will turn kids off and reinforce any negative feelings they have about books to begin with.

There is an art to putting the right book in the hand of the right reader. Choosing inaccessible reading materials will, again, turn off a teen who doesn't like to read. This means asking careful questions about the reader's interests—and disinterests. Books that look hard to read should be avoided unless you can *really* sell them. If, as you are pitching a book to a kid, you hear for yourself how boring it sounds, put it aside. That said, just because a teen is not responding enthusiastically to you doesn't mean they're not listening or interested. Teens are not always the most demonstrative patrons in the library. Give the reader's advisory conversation time and patience.

Don't stereotype. Not all girls like chick lit; not all boys like sports stories. Easy to say, less easy to do. Ask questions! Use the guide in the next section as your template.

Remember, books aren't the only reading material out there. Making this clear to teens and their parents and educators can take a bit of work on your part, but it is a crucial point. Teens who spend time online are reading. Teens who flip though magazines are reading. Teens who play video games are reading—have you ever seen how much text there is in those adventure game cut scenes? And even if we are just talking about books, not all books need be fiction books. Some of the best books out there for reluctant readers are picture-heavy nonfiction books. Some of those are listed here and are marked with (NF); I have also included a list of all nonfiction books at the end.

Series books

Divine, L. *Drama High* series

Kaye, Marilyn. *Gifted* series

Lee, Darrien. *Denim Diaries* series

Mead, Richelle. *Vampire Academy* series

Millner, Denene and Mitzi Miller. *Hotlanta* series

Singleton, Linda Joy. *Dead Girl Walking* series

Vampires and the paranormal

Brewer, Heather. The *Vladimir Todd* series

Garcia, Kami and Margaret Stohl. *Beautiful Creatures* and *Beautiful Darkness*

Klause, Annette Curtis. *Blood and Chocolate*

Noel, Alison. The *Immortals* series

Perez, Marlene. *Dead Is So Last Year, Dead Is the New Black, Dead Is Just a Rumor,* and *Dead is a State of Mind*

Reisz, Kristopher. *Unleashed*

Schroeder, Lisa. *I Heart You, You Haunt Me*

Smith, L. J. The *Vampire Diaries* series

Stiefvater, Maggie. *Shiver*

Romance

Cabot, Meg. *All-American Girl*

Davidson, Dana. *Jason and Keira*

Dessen, Sarah. *This Lullaby*

Elkeles, Simone. *Perfect Chemistry*

Garden, Nancy. *Annie on My Mind*

Sones, Sonya. *What My Mother Doesn't Know* and *What My Girlfriend Doesn't Know*

Van Draanen, Wendelin. *Flipped*

Funny books

Bauer, Joan. *Thwonk*

Garza, Mario. *Stuff on My Cat: The Book* (NF)

Henderson, Alan. *Mullet Madness! The Haircut That's Business Up Front and a Party in the Back* (NF)

Korman, Gordon. *Son of the Mob*

Limb, Sue. *Girl, 15, Charming but Insane*

Miller, Kerry. *Passive Aggressive Notes: Painfully Polite and Hilariously Hostile Writings* (NF)

Rennison. Louise. The *Georgia Nicholson* series

Turner, Tracy. *The 70s: The Decade that Style Forgot* (NF)

Nonfiction books

Blackshaw, Ric and Farrelly, Liz. *Street Art Book: 60 Artists in Their Own Words*

Blasberg, Derek. *Classy: Exceptional Advice for the Extremely Modern Lady*

Bright, J. E. *America's Next Top Model: Fierce Guide to Life: The Ultimate Source of Beauty, Fashion, and Model Behavior*

Bush, Jenna. *Ana's Story: A Journal of Hope*

Canfield, Jack. *Chicken Soup for the Teenage Soul: 101 Stories of Life, Love, Learning*

D'Arcy, Sean. *Freestyle Soccer Tricks*

Hardwicke, Catherine. *Twilight Director's Notebook: The Story of How We Made the Movie*

Hopkins, Jerry and Danny Sugarman. *No One Here Gets Out Alive*

Kidder, Lisa Damian. *Glee: Totally Unofficial, The Ultimate Guide to the Smash-Hit High School Musical*

Kuklin, Susan. *No Choirboy: Murder, Violence, and Teenagers on Death Row*

Seventeen Magazine. *Mega Traumarama! Real Girls and Guys Confess More of Their Most Mortifying Moments!*

Sheff, Nic. *Tweak: Growing up on Methamphetamines*

Vibe Magazine. *Tupac Shakur*

Graphic novels

Abadzis, Nick. *Laika*

Ashihara, Hinako. *Sand Chronicles* series

Friedman, Aimee. *Breaking Up: A Fashion High Graphic Novel*

Loux, Matthew. *Sidescrollers*

Meyer, Stephenie. *Twilight: The Graphic Novel*

Miller, Frank. *Batman: The Dark Knight Returns*

Mizushiro, Setona. *After School Nightmare* series

Reger, Rob and Gruner, Jessica. *Emily the Strange: The Lost Days*

Smith, Jeff. *Bone: Out from Boneville*

Sad/problem books

Anonymous. *Go Ask Alice*

Booth, Coe. *Tyrell*

Brown, Jennifer. *Hate List*

Forman, Gail. *If I Stay*

Hopkins, Ellen. *Crank*

McCormick, Patricia. *Cut*

McDaniel, Lurlene. *Don't Die, My Love*

Pelzer, Dave. *A Child Called It: One Child's Courage to Survive* (NF)

Ryan, Darlene. *Five Minutes More*

Zarr, Sara. *Story of a Girl*

HOMEWORK COLLECTIONS: YEA OR NAY?

As a school librarian, I spent most of my budget on nonfiction books that supported the collection. A plethora of publishers put out series non-fiction books that are specifically targeted to high school research areas: pro/con books, current events, country profiles, social issues, and the like. These books prove extremely useful to students who are writing papers or presentations, though they are usually better suited to younger teens or lower-level classes, as older teens or those in more advanced classes tend to look to primary sources and adult nonfiction for their research needs.

When it was time to buy books for the teen area at Darien Library, I care-fully considered whether or not these or other nonfiction titles should be included in the collection. To answer that question, I had to decide what the mission of the teen collection was. I took the following things into consideration, and I suggest you do the same in making this decision for your own space:

Size of the space. How big is the room you're filling? How many linear feet of shelf space do you have? If the teen area is on the small side, you will have to carefully consider how much precious shelf space you want to designate for a homework collection. The size of the space also determines how versatile it will be, as further on, in the "What is the teen space going to be used for?" section.

The adult collection. Are there materials in the adult collection that can be used for high school and middle school research projects? Chances are, the reference librarians have been buying books that support certain recurrent research needs, though I suspect they are not the type of series nonfiction books that I described earlier, but rather adult books. Most adult services librarians do not collect series nonfiction as they can eat up a large chunk of the budget and cannot really be borrowed by anyone but high school students, once a year—so they don't get as much bang for the buck as one might like. Which brings us to our third criteria.

The book budget. If it's small, or even if it's a medium-sized budget that has to cover a lot of ground in building a new collection, then how much money do you want to devote to a homework collection? Will you be able to support every research project, or just one? Will you be able to update these often time-sensitive titles as often as is necessary?

The high school collection. Talk to the local high school librarian about what she has to offer her students. I would not be surprised if most of the books needed to support recurring research projects are already in her collection. That said, there may be some areas that she has been meaning to bulk up but she doesn't have the funds to do so. Talk specifics—is there one particular project that she just wishes she could support?

Your library's databases. If teens in your community have been educated about databases—and, for that matter, if their teachers have, too—then they can use articles found through databases to fulfill their research requirements. Check out what you've got. You won't be able to tell if your databases support every project that's going to come through the library, but you can ask the research librarians in your library if they think the databases cover enough ground. Again, speak to the school librarians to try to build a rudimentary list of annual research projects that they are aware of, and then spend some time in the databases to see if there are any gaps. These gaps could be filled by books or they could be filled by more databases. It depends on what teachers are asking for and how comfortable the teens in your community are with using databases.

What is the teen space going to be used for? This is, perhaps, the most important question. What do you intend teens to do with the teen space? How do you envision it looking? Do you picture teens bent over their notebooks, working in study groups, and using the computers to look up information for their assignments? Or do you envision it as a noisier space, with video games competing with YouTube videos and teens reading magazines and catching up with their friends? Of course, a space doesn't have to be just one of these things—usage changes throughout the day and differs from weekday to weekend. But if your space is small, without different zones or areas where teens can choose to be either studious or noisy without disturbing or being disturbed by your teens, then you will have to resign yourself to the fact that a space might just be one thing or the other. It's a chicken-and-egg question, though: if you buy homework books and load databases onto the computers, teens may decide to use the room as a study space; if you don't hook up printers and sacrifice nonfiction for magazines, then it might be a hangout space. If you can, watch how the space is used for a little while before you make any decisions. There is no point in buying resources on either end of the spectrum for teens who won't use them. Your money is best spent on the materials that are in the highest demand, especially if you are working with limited funds.

What I Did

I did not purchase a homework collection, mainly because I intended the teen room, which was small, to be a hangout space. This decision was based on several factors. One, teens in Darien were already accustomed to using the adult nonfiction collection for their research needs. Older teens especially—those who were most likely to be assigned research projects—used the reference room almost exclusively. Younger teens—those who were still working from textbooks—tended to use the teen lounge. The teen room was too small to be used to do homework at any but the quietest times. To satisfy the younger teens who *did* want to do homework and who found the teen lounge too distracting, we reserved a conference room once a week to provide a homework space. In order to make this appealing, we offered snacks, school supplies, and help with homework.

However, if I had ever heard that teens were not able to find the information that they needed to do their homework in the library, I would have found a way to start purchasing more nonfiction books for the teen lounge. The teen lounge did offer nonfiction, but it was all high-interest: humor, photography, how-tos, beauty, crafts, relationships, mental health, and so on. We did have some high-interest memoirs and biographies that were occasionally used for research, but for the most part, we sent teens to the adult collection for this purpose.

PROMOTING THE COLLECTION

Displaying materials drives circulation up, up, up. There are a few reasons why you might want to display books or other materials: you want to increase the circulation of books that aren't being checked out as much as you would like; you want to make it easier for teens to find the most popular books; you want to highlight new books and other materials; or you want to call attention to a certain group of books based on a theme. Tying the collection to programs or certain times of the year (including advocacy events like Teen Read Week, among others) is a great way to promote the collection and promote literacy. If, for example, you are running a craft workshop, displaying materials that relate to crafts could be a way to connect teens with books they might not have known about or checked out without promotion. See Chapter 2 for information on display furniture.

Display Ideas

There are a few basic ways of making a display effective. First, make sure that the display is in a high-traffic area, if possible. Somewhere by the door is good, or near something else in the room that is a draw: the computers, the TV, the Online Public Access Catalog, or something similar. If there is a staff desk in the room where you check out books, place items on display there so that teens will look at them as they wait. Second, use signage. Make signs clear, clean, and easy to read. Use bold, large, simple fonts and print signs in colors that are attractive and complementary. Because we're talking about teens, you may want to try to use trendy colors (neons, for example), but make sure that the sign can be read from across the room and is not too busy or uses clashing colors. Third, include recommendations with the displayed materials. This can be as simple as making the theme of the display "staff recommends" or "teens recommend," or it can mean tucking a bookmark into each item with a mini-review attached. Finally, keep it fresh. If books aren't going out, change them up after a week or so. After that, the books become part of the furniture and no one will notice them anymore. And when a book does get grabbed, replace its empty spot with a new one.

There are a few ways to create eye-catching, unique displays that will draw teens' attention to the materials you're highlighting. For example:

- Themes. There are so many to choose from; read the section following for some ideas.

- Colors. Put out only books with green covers, black covers, etc. Or a combination—red and pink for valentine's day, orange, brown and red for the first day of fall.

- Teen-selected. Ask your TAB or any other group or individual to pull their favorites and place them out. Make sure it's clear that teens chose the books, since that in and of itself can be a huge selling point. Another way to do this is to put out slips of paper for teens to write reviews on and stick into books, which they can then put on display.

- Voting. If you're taking part in YALSA's Teens' Top 10, a component of Teen Read Week, put all the copies out so that teens can take them home and vote. Or, create your own battle of the books. Make sure you put ballots out with the books.

- Tied to programs or town-wide events. One way to make books instantly appealing is to give them context. This can be anything you like—a gaming program, a movie screening, an open mic night. Or, expand your focus beyond library programs and think about community interests and goings-on. Is there a big sports tournament coming up, or an arts festival? What's happening in the news? School events like graduation, prom, and the first day of classes are always easy tie-ins, and keep an eye on community calendars for other ideas, too.

Themes

There are so many potential display themes that this will only be a small sampling of the possibilities. Definitely think about what will be of interest to the teens who use your library and the things that make your community special.

- Seasons. Sure, there's fall, summer, spring, and winter, but what about mud season, which is a real thing in northern New England? Or the beginning of baseball season? There are also specific season-related themes like spring break, school's out, end of summer, the winter blues, Indian summers, and so on.

- Holidays. Pick the nondenominational ones (Thanksgiving, Valentine's Day, Fourth of July) and don't get too cheesy. A fun thing to do with holiday displays is to create a bulletin board with a question written on it in big letters: "Who's your valentine?" or "What are you going to dress up as for Halloween?" Put out construction paper shapes that are related to the holiday and a bunch of markers. When teens fill out their answers, staple them to the bulletin board. You would be surprised how much even high school students love to do this.

- Teen-created. Have your teens pick the theme and then pick the books. Have them make some signs to go along with the display so that teens know it's peer created and the theme is nice and clear.

- Genres. There are always the basics, like funny books and fantasy books, but you also might have fun picking out more specific genres, like fairy books, dark humor, werewolves, girl detectives, buddy comedies, sea adventures, dystopia, or tear-jerkers.

- Colors. Believe it or not, this is a great way to catch the eye. Base your colors upon a certain seasonal theme (red, white, and blue in the summer; the high school's official colors in the fall; pink in February) or just because. Color-based displays look great. A rainbow could also be fun.

- New arrivals and hottest titles. Use your ILS to pull the popular data—which books have gone out the most in the past month—and pull a selection of new books from every shipment to display.

- Movie and TV tie-ins. Once a book becomes a show, it's sure to get some more buzz. Here are some examples:
  - *The Vampire Diaries* (TV)
  - *Pretty Little Liars* (TV)
  - *The Boy in the Striped Pajamas* (Movie)
  - *The Golden Compass* (Movie)
  - *Cirque du Freak* (Movie)
  - *The Princess Diaries* (Movie)
  - *Gossip Girl* (TV)
  - *The Carrie Diaries* (TV)

- Book pairs. Couple a hot new book with an older favorite that has the same theme:
  - Pair a book with a book discussed by the first book's characters: Pair *King Dork* by Frank Portman with *The Catcher in the Rye* by J. D. Salinger; *Eclipse* by Stephenie Meyer with *Wuthering Heights* by Charlotte Brontë.
  - Modern interpretations of Shakespeare: Pair *Hamlet: A Novel* by John Marsden with *Hamlet; Romiette and Julio* by Sharon Draper with *Romeo and Juliet*.

OBSTACLES IN COLLECTION DEVELOPMENT
Budget Limitations and Decisions

As mentioned, if you are low on budget you will have to make choices about how to spend your money. Budgets can be all over the map, from those under a thousand dollars to those in the tens of thousands. No matter the budget, you can never buy everything you'd like to buy, and you will always have to make choices—but it goes without saying that the smaller the budget, the more choices you have to make. So again, get back to your goals. What do you want the teen collection to accomplish? Are you focused mostly on buying books that will circulate heavily, or is it more important to reach the broadest range of teens possible? Do you want to collect mostly popular fiction, or do you want to be sure that the niche books are well-represented? If you have done any analysis of circulation prior to your arrival, and if you have talked to as many teens as possible about their reading interests, then you should have a decent sense of what teens are looking for. And with any luck, you already have a collection of some shape—the books you have culled from other areas of the library, as discussed earlier in this section.

So for the purposes of illustration, let's say you have $1,000 to purchase books (other materials not included). This is a small budget when you consider that books, even when purchased from large vendors, cost about $10 a pop—sometimes less and sometimes more, of course, based on whether they're paperback or hardcover. If the average price is $10, though, you can buy about 100 books. How the heck are you going to spend this money? You have to stretch your $1,000 the best you can and make very good choices.

You might divide up the money based on percentages. 50 percent of what you buy will be realistic fiction, 20 percent will be fantasy, 10 percent will be series fiction, 5 percent will be historical fiction, 5 percent will be science fiction, and 5 percent will be nonfiction. These numbers can be linked to your circulation statistics or based on analysis of the current collection or other library collections.

Another method would be to purchase a certain amount of books from lists—YALSA's Best Fiction for Young Adults (BFYA), for example—and save the rest for new books throughout the year and patron requests. This would mean that you had a certain amount to spread throughout the rest of the year, for purchases based on reviews in the journals. In this $1,000 example, if you bought 20 books based on BBYA, you would have roughly

$800 left to divide over the course of the following year—maybe 7 or 8 books a month. All these numbers sound very small, so you will have to carefully consider the reviews every month and try to determine:

1. Is there an audience for this book? Can I think of one or two teens who might be interested in this book?
2. Is this book at the right reading level for the teens in my community?
3. Is the topic of interest to teens in my community?
4. Has there been a request for this book?
5. Is this book a sequel to a title that was very popular?

Ways to Get Cheap Books

If your administration allows it, there are venues for more inexpensive books than are offered via the big vendors. Used books are an option, although not entirely desirable. If you choose this approach, make sure they're in very good condition. The consolation is that because teen books usually only stay popular for a short time, it's OK to buy copies that won't last forever.

- Publisher warehouse sales. Scholastic has several warehouses that offer huge sales. Go to http://www.scholastic.com/bookfairs/events/warehouse/ to find locations and sale events. Searching for *publisher warehouse sales* on Google will get you a whole host of results for publishers in your area that are hosting sales at their warehouses.

- Used book stores. You must either have a corporate credit card to do this or feel comfortable being reimbursed, but you can purchase books with deep discounts this way. Just make sure they are new and in good condition. And don't buy a book just because it's cheap. Buy it because you would buy it anyway, new or used.

- Library books sales. Yes—this may seem weird, but large libraries that are shedding books will often be selling multiple copies, which means you can find new and popular titles for very, very low prices. Again, you would need to feel comfortable being reimbursed, if this is even an option at your library. Additionally, colleges often have massive book sales, such as the one at Bryn Mawr every March (http://bmandwbooks.com/). Check your local colleges to see if they do anything similar.

- Online used book vendors. When searching for books on Amazon, see what the outside vendors are offering. Other sites to check are alibris.com, bookfinder.com, powells.com, and half.ebay.com. Many of these vendors will accept American Express, which solves the whole reimbursement problem. But remember that you will have to pay for shipping.
- Discount stores. Big box stores like Walmart and Costco sell books cheaply and will stock popular titles. You may be able to pick up multiple copies of bestsellers at cut rates.

Space Limitations

Finding enough room for your books is an issue in small rooms or hallways or nooks or whatever it is that you've got. You will have to make tough choices based on linear feet of shelving. If you've got a budget but no room, I have one word for you: weeding. Do not be afraid of it. Weeding is your friend. Once you've got your core collection all set up, monitor it closely. Make books earn their keep. If they aren't circulating, they go on display, and if they still aren't circulating, they're out the door. This makes room for new books that will circ.

Avoid multiple copies if you can, but choose a multiple copy of a super-popular title over a single copy of a mediocre or low-interest title. Collection development is a fine balance between buying popular, often-requested books and niche books that are of extremely high interest to a very small group. With limited space, this becomes an even more delicate balancing act.

Don't forget that books leave the library shelves. So you can own more books than you can fit on the shelf. You will find that the shelves are stuffed to the gills during some months and bare in others (typically the summer strips all books from the library, while the winter fills them all back up). If you have storage space available to you in the library, put multiple copies there and use them to restock when demand gets higher.

Think about alternative shelving solutions. Paperback spinners can be used for nonprint materials like DVDs, CDs, and video games, or for particular collections if they fit. There are shelves that can be fitted to the ends of other shelves or to pillars. Have shelving retrofitted to any wall space you can. Magazines don't have to be housed in traditional magazine shelving; they can go into boxes or be displayed on tables, with older issues living in storage or tucked away somewhere in the space.

Challenges to the Collection

It is a rare library that does not experience a challenge to the collection; there's a good chance this could happen to you. Young adult books tend to get targeted more than others because they often contain mature content for readers under the age of eighteen. When I was a school librarian, the *Gossip Girl* series was challenged by a parent whose sixth-grader, age 11, brought one of the books in the series home. Because librarians are not *in loco parentis,* it is not our responsibility to dictate what materials are appropriate for certain children and teens. That is up to the readers—and in some cases their parents—to decide. A teen collection is used by a broad range of readers, both in age, maturity, and education, and it is the responsibility of the teen librarian to collect materials that are appropriate for that broad range. This means that some of the books in the collection may not be appropriate for some of the readers who use the space. So what happens when the wrong material, book or otherwise, gets in the hands of a teen and, as a result, the material is challenged?

The number-one way to deal with challenges to the collection is to be prepared, and the number-one way to be prepared is to have a collection development policy, which is discussed in detail in this chapter. When you are approached, either face-to-face, over the phone, or via e-mail, it is your job to listen to the complainant. Do not immediately dismiss the person or get defensive. Oftentimes, people just want to be heard, and doing something as simple as listening could stop the complaint dead in its tracks. This is a subtle action, however, as you don't want to cede anything to the person complaining—"I agree, that book *is* inappropriate!"— but you also don't want to shut them down right away, either. Sometimes it can be as simple as saying "I understand what you're saying." Be an active listener and do not dismiss the person out of hand. (It might be worth asking your director or direct supervisor for advice on this, as chances are they have dealt with a similar situation at some point during their careers.)

You might explain the library's policy on collecting materials and make the point that I did above, which is that the teen collection is provided for teens who are at varying ages and maturity levels. I have found that some people understand this and some do not. You may be asked to restrict the materials in some way by putting a label on them, keeping them in the back office, or shelving in a special area. At this point, you will have to explain that doing so is restricting the materials, which is against the library's policy (if such a policy exists). This may be the point when a patron decides to formally challenge the material, because you're essentially not budging on the issue. And I should make the point that throughout this process, you should keep your director in the loop. This is much easier to do if this exchange is taking place via e-mail; if you are having a face-to-face conversation, let your director know at the earliest possible moment about the conversation so that he or she can both be aware and give you guidance if necessary.

If the patron decides to make a formal challenge to the collection, either by filling out a form (if available) or sending a letter or making a direct in-person request to the director, the board, or some other administrative body, then chances are the matter will no longer be your responsibility, but become that of the director or library board. Once the issue is turned over to them, you will probably be involved in some way, though you will not be the main decision maker in the outcome.

It's worth noting that the anticipation of challenges should not be a factor in your acquisitions decisions. You should be aware of the needs and interests of your community, but if those needs lead you toward materials that could be controversial, you should not shy away from purchasing them because a patron might find them upsetting. And this idea runs both ways—you should also not collect controversial materials if your community is not interested in such things. It's hard, sometimes, to reconcile your personal interests and philosophies with the needs of the community if they are vastly different. If you are the only conservative in a town with a liberal bent, it may be hard to purchase books that are not to your political taste. Or, if your community tends to be fairly conservative, you may not want to spend a lot of money on books with graphic sex talk. Just remember: this isn't because you're trying to avoid a challenge, it's because these materials aren't going to be of high interest to your readers. I am loath to even write about this because it is *such* a fine line, and some might argue that books about sex and other sensitive topics will always be of interest to teens, no matter how religious/straitlaced a community is. Those who argue as much might make the case that while these books won't get checked out, they will get read, either in the library or by teens who borrow books without actually checking them out. To that end, read the section below about honor baskets. Navigating this fine line can be easier if you are not the only person making purchasing decisions. But, of course, this can be tricky if you are the only teen librarian. All libraries are different, and all library directors handle collection issues differently, so it bears repeating that it is always a good idea to discuss all of this with your director.

Resources That Can Help

Because challenges to the collection take place so frequently, there are numerous resources available to librarians online. The American Library Association devotes a great deal of its resources to intellectual freedom and censorship issues, and it pays particular attention to supporting librarians who experience challenges. You may find the following resources helpful if you are one such librarian, though it is worth looking these over before it comes to that.

- The ALA Office for Intellectual Freedom (OIF) is a warehouse of information (http://www.ala.org/ala/aboutala/offices/oif/index.cfm), including:
  - The very helpful Intellectual Freedom toolkits (http://www.ala.org/ala/aboutala/offices/oif/iftoolkits/intellectual.cfm)
  - Collections of state laws
  - The complete text of the USA PATRIOT Act
  - Strategies for coping with challenges (http://www.ala.org/ala/issuesadvocacy/banned/challengeslibrarymaterials/copingwithchallenges/index.cfm).
  - The OIF has several online presences, including on Facebook, Twitter, and YouTube, and has a special section devoted to intellectual freedom and social networks (http://www.ala.org/ala/aboutala/offices/oif/ifissues/onlinesocialnetworks.cfm)
  - Finally, the OIF specifically addresses the issue of youth and libraries at http://www.lita.org/ala/issuesadvocacy/banned/challengeslibrarymaterials/essentialpreparation/kidslibraries/index.cfm, which is essential reading.
- The Library Bill of Rights http://staging.ala.org/ala/aboutala/offices/oif/statementspols/statementsif/librarybillrights.cfm) is a clear, concise document that was written in 1948. It has been amended a few times since and there are several interpretations of the bill for different audiences and service groups. These interpretations (http://staging.ala.org/ala/aboutala/offices/oif/statementspols/statementsif/interpretations/default.cfm) include a few that will be of special interest to teen librarians:
  - Access for Children and Young Adults to Nonprint Materials: http://staging.ala.org/ala/aboutala/offices/oif/statementspols/statementsif/interpretations/accesschildren.cfm

- Access to Resources and Services in the School Library Media Program: http://staging.ala.org/ala/aboutala/offices/oif/statement spols/statementsif/interpretations/accessresources.cfm
  - Free Access to Libraries for Minors: http://staging.ala.org/ala/aboutala/offices/oif/statementspols/statementsif/interpretations/freeaccesslibraries.cfm
  - Restricted Access to Library Materials: http://staging.ala.org/ala/aboutala/offices/oif/statementspols/statementsif/interpretations/restrictedaccess.cfm
- YALSA offers advice specifically related to young adult materials at http://www.lita.org/ala/mgrps/divs/yalsa/profdev/yachallenges.cfm. This includes links to other libraries' collection development policies and a section devoted just to graphic novels.
- Speaking of graphic novels, the Comic Book Legal Defense Fund (http://cbldf.org/), a nonprofit organization founded in 1986 to pay for the legal defense of a comic book store manager charged with distributing obscenity, is worth a look if you collect graphic novels or comics for teens. As I write this, the site does not offer any resources, but it does contain information on past cases and press releases that are interesting reading.
- Banned Books Week (http://www.bannedbooksweek.org/) is more an advocacy and educational tool than anything else. Some libraries shy away from promoting this annual event as it can call attention to questionable materials in a library's collection, while others see it as an opportunity to educate teens and their parents about how censorship and book banning can be harmful, as some of the most-banned books are surprising additions to the list.

Theft

Theft is an issue no matter where your library is located. Teens don't just steal books because they can't afford to buy them, and missing books are not always the result of intentional stealing. Even if your library has a security system, there are ways of getting books out the door without setting off any alarms. So what can you do? Sit in the teen area and watch the teens like a hawk to make sure no one stuffs anything in his backpack? Well, no—you can't; you don't have time, and that isn't a very good way of showing the teens that you trust them. A few intentional acts of thievery should not reflect on all of your teen patrons.

Some libraries figure out which books are being stolen and keep those items behind a desk or in a back office, so that teens have to ask for them. The logic behind this is that the teen will not steal the item because the librarian knows who they are when they hand the book over. This may be true, but it's far worse to restrict certain materials—and essentially make them unavailable to teens—than it is to run the risk of the item being stolen.

Instead, I suggest two other tactics. One, make sure you have built replacement costs into your budget. After a year or two, you should have a pretty good idea of how many books you need to replace in a given year. Sometimes, you won't replace a book that's been stolen, just like you sometimes don't replace books that are withdrawn because of wear and tear. But you will want to replace a certain percentage, and you should make sure that you can afford to do that, accepting that certain books are just going to walk out the door, and there's nothing you can do about it.

Two, I suggest considering the idea of the honor basket. This idea is not mine but rather that of Valerie Diggs, the amazing Department Head of Libraries for the District of Chelmsford, Massachusetts. I attended one of Valerie's classes at Simmons and fell in love with the idea of the honor basket. Basically, Valerie recommends taking books on sensitive topics— sex, drugs, body image, sexuality, health, divorce, bullying, and the like— and removing them from the catalog. These books then go into special baskets scattered throughout the teen area or school library in discreet places, where teens can feel comfortable browsing through them. A sign indicates that teens may borrow these books and return them whenever they like, and that they do not need to be checked out. Some of the books will never come back, of course, but I believe that a large number of books stolen from the library are taken because the teen does not feel comfortable bringing the book to the circulation desk. By eliminating that part of the process, teens may feel more comfortable borrowing and then bringing back the book.

Keeping Fresh and Keeping Up, Especially on a Limited Budget

Collection development can be overwhelming and stressful, especially as the number of books published for teens continues to grow. We have all been in the position where we realize there are several popular books that have been published within the last few months that are not on our shelves. It's very easy to let things slip between the cracks, but there are a few ways to keep up with new releases and to focus on what's most important.

Book Expo America (BEA) is the annual publishing conference and exposition held in New York City every May. BEA is an excellent place to meet authors, get advanced copies of new titles, and see publisher exhibits. If you visit BEA, make sure to spend time speaking with the representatives from different publishing houses. Ask them to tell you which books you should pay particular attention to. Which books are going to have big print runs and heavy-duty publicity campaigns? Also try to grab advance reading copies. These bound galleys are uncorrected proofs of upcoming books and reading them is a great way to have a sense of which books to pitch to your teens. They also make a great prize giveaway, especially if they're signed.

BEA may be out of your price range, especially if you're not in the northeast, but that doesn't mean you can't connect with publishers in other ways. Visit teen publisher websites. Many of them have excellent tools for keeping up-to-date on their catalog, in addition to offering extra features for teens and librarians alike.

Harper Teen—http://www.harperteen.com/. Sign up for the *Hip Lit* newsletter, follow @harperteen for giveaways and promotions, have your teens sign up for contests, check out book trailers on YouTube, and sign up for Harper's Author Tracker (http://www.harpercollins.com/members/authortracker/).

Random House Teen—http://www.randomhouse.com/teens/. Send teens to Random Buzzers, Random House's online community for teen readers (http://www.randombuzzers.com/), sign up for newsletters, have teens sign up for giveaways, visit the Author's Corner, and browse through new releases.

Penguin Young Readers—http://us.penguingroup.com/teens. Includes many imprints. Browse new releases, visit sites for different series and stand-alone titles, sign up for the newsletter, send teens to the Point of View/TeenNick site to discuss their favorites on the message board and watch book trailers (http://www.teennick.com/trends/sponsors/penguin/).

Bloomsbury Teen—http://www.bloomsburykids.com/books/teen. Find new releases, award winners, and coming soon books, watch book trailers, get reading group guides, and sign up for the newsletter.

Macmillan Children and Teens—http://us.macmillan.com/macmillan site/categories/Childrens/Macmillan/TopSellers. Includes a huge number of imprints. Find best sellers, browse by category, find activity and discussion guides, sign up for the newsletter.

Scholastic—http://www.scholastic.com/kids. The site is for both children and teens. Play games, browse popular series and authors, read the blog (http://blog.scholastic.com/), watch videos, and comment on the message boards.

Reach out to publishers to see if they have a library contact who can occasionally apprise you of upcoming releases, let you know if authors are in the area, and send you advance reading copies. Publishers that provide ARCs like to know that they are being read and reviewed by teens, so if you can, pass along feedback to the reps that they can use. If you pass along an ARC to a teen, you can have them fill out a brief review form that could then be popped into the mail or scanned and e-mailed.

Early Word (http://www.earlyword.com/) is a blog created by Nora Rawlinson to keep librarians up to date on publishing news. Rawlinson is a librarian who was also the editor-in-chief of *Publishers Weekly* for 12 years. *Early Word* caters mostly to librarians purchasing adult materials, though it does have a healthy children's and YA section, which can be found here: http://www.earlyword.com/category/childrens-and-ya/. Visit *Early Word* for great information about upcoming books, top sellers, best-of lists, and buzz.

Additionally, there are a few sites you can add to your feed reader to help you keep up on pub dates. One is YALit.com (http://www.yalit.com/), a bare bones list of teen book releases, both upcoming and recently published. The *School Library Journal* newsletter *SLJ Teen* is similar—it highlights upcoming and recent books, plus adds a bit of publishing and library news. And finally (but not *really* finally, since there are so many blogs out there that it's impossible to list them all), there is Teens Read Too (http://www.teensreadtoo.com/), which publishes teen-written reviews of newly released books every month, at http://www.teensreadtoo.com/BookReviews.html.

Throughout the ongoing process of collection development, it's most important to keep in mind that building a teen collection is just that: a process. You will most certainly purchase books that you think look great but will never circulate, and the books you didn't give a second glance to will fly off the shelf, resulting in a panicked trip to the local bookstore to get additional copies. You will buy books of a sensitive nature, hoping that they will get into the hands of those who most need them, only to find a bunch of teens sitting around laughing at the table of contents. You will also hear from parents who think a book doesn't belong in the collection, either because it's not high-quality enough or downright inappropriate or offensive. Placing the responsibility on one librarian to satisfy the needs and standards of all teen readers (and, as much as we don't like to admit it, the adults in their lives) is fairly unrealistic. We all have our own biases, pet interests, and ham-fisted desires to promote a certain kind of book. It's silly to say otherwise. All we can do is try to be objective, keep the needs of the community foremost in our mind, and be quick on our feet. Do that, and you will curate an excellent collection.

NOTE

1. Graphic novels are not really a genre in and of themselves, so you may choose to shelve graphic novels according to their topic's genre. At Darien Library, I chose to shelve them separately because it made them easy for readers to browse them, and I found that graphic novel readers liked to have all of them in one place. I shelved manga and traditional graphic novels in the same place.

4

◇ ◇ ◇

PROGRAMMING

Programming is *fun*. It's why being a teen librarian is so great. Sometimes you might have to pinch yourself—you get to watch *Gossip Girl* for work? Or mess around on the computer on the clock? You can play video games during the workday and not get in trouble with your boss? Yes. If you're a teen librarian, you get to play, too.

This chapter addresses the best way to start the process of building programs that teens will enjoy and be attracted to, strategies for getting creative tools into the hands of teens, and the logistics of program planning. That includes publicity, partnering with others in the community, and getting teens involved in the planning process.

There's no point in rushing into anything, as eager as you might be. You've got to get to know your community before you can really start programming. On the flip side of that coin, you'll never learn about what works if you don't try. So start slowly and be patient. Give programs time to blossom. We held a chess program four times before anyone came at all, and now we get a steady, regular crowd each week. It's worth the wait— but it's also important to know when to throw in the towel.

By now, I've told you repeatedly to learn about what the teens in your community are into. Just like it helps with collection development, it also helps with program planning. So talk to the teens, read the paper, and gather information from your colleagues. Is there a focus in your community on sports? The arts? Music? Pop culture? Do most kids work after high school, or go to college? How focused are they on that? Don't lump everyone together, but you should program based on demand. I once discovered that, despite my claims that knitting was *so* over, a group of girls was meeting every Saturday in the library to knit together. I asked them if I could make it a library program and invite others to join, and they said sure! Easy peasy library program. You may find that teens are already hanging out at the library and doing something together, whether it's playing computer games, studying for AP tests, or just lounging around and reading magazines. Whatever it is, borrow their idea and expand on it.

Conversely, there's something to be said for creating programs that fill a void. In a sporty town, maybe there aren't enough creative opportunities for the teens who don't want to play lacrosse. In a town where not a lot of kids go to Ivy Leagues, maybe there are some teens who would just like to get together and work on their college essays together. You'll start getting hints from teens if you're hanging around them enough in the library. Parents are another great source of information. "I wish there was somewhere my son could learn more computer skills" is something I once heard from a mom. Well, the library had the computers and the willing staff—so we could make something happen.

Remember: excellent programming happens when librarians can turn on a dime, take a risk, and dive into something new and maybe even uncomfortable. Your own interests are not necessarily the same as the teens' in your community. What matters more is that you show you're listening. So it's OK to admit you kinda don't like anime, as long as you say it as you're planning a film festival for the teens who do. Or if you always thought teen programming was about crafts, TV shows, and gaming, you might have to swallow your pride and create a couple of boring college admissions events after no one comes to the craft programs.

PROGRAMMING IDEAS
Gaming

Gaming is the guaranteed crowd-pleaser. Boys and girls love it. It's relatively easy, if expensive, to pull off. Why put on gaming events? They're fun, they bring teens to the library who might not come in otherwise, and gaming supports a whole host of benefits. These benefits are discussed in greater detail later in this chapter, but here are some basic ideas:

- National Gaming Day Tournament. Visit http://www.ilovelibrar ies.org/gaming/ to learn more about this event, which takes place every November. You'll need a Wii and an Internet connection, plus someone at your library who feels comfortable with networking stuff (although I'm told it's pretty basic). On NGD, teams from all over the country compete against each other in *Super Smash Bros. Brawl*. It's a great way to build community spirit—a little light-hearted trash talking between towns never hurts anyone—and it's a cool way to connect your teens with the wider world.

- In-house tournaments. Super easy to pull off. All you need is a bracket and a prize. Good games to run tourneys with are the aforementioned *Super Smash Bros. Brawl, Mario Kart,* and *Rock Band*. It's also fun to put on *American Idol*-like games. Just sub-stitute "American" with the name of your town/branch/school. The *American Idol* game scores each player, so it's easy to have one winner come out on top just by recording the scores. Videotape the event and post it online (with teen permission) for a lovely example of the talent and good humor among your teens.

- Free-for-all gaming. If you can, keep games out after school and let teens just play when they want. It can be a great way for them to blow off steam. It also shows that you trust them and that not every-thing has to be managed by an adult. A word of warning: sometimes video games can dominate the use of a space, so it's worth either limiting the amount of time that teens can play games or only mak-ing games available that are fun for teens of all ages and genders to play. *Halo* can absolutely drive all the girls out of the room and keep boys from doing anything but play. *Wii Fit* is a great one to have around. It appeals to girls and boys, promotes good health, and isn't very disruptive to other teens in the room who aren't gaming.

Reviewing and Purchasing Games and Gaming Systems

Before you can purchase a gaming system, your space needs to be equipped with a television. It doesn't have to be the biggest, fanciest TV around, but a fairly large one that is high-definition compatible would be best, for the quality of the graphics and the comfort of the players. It is pos-sible to use a TV on a cart, so if there is already one in your library that you can use whenever possible, you will not have to purchase a new TV. If you do have to purchase a TV, try to find one that is at least 27 inches. This is large enough for a group of teens to sit around and play at once. Flat screens are lighter, easier to move, and able to be mounted to the wall, but are more expensive. Check big box stores and discount electronics stores for the best deals, or ask someone on the technology staff for help—they may be able to purchase equipment at a discount through a library vendor or consortium. If you do go into a store, ask the salesperson for advice. Explain that you will be hooking up gaming systems to the television; they will be able to ensure that you have all of the necessary connections and options.

With all of the video games out in the world, it might be tough to know where to start with creating a new lending or gaming program. It will help to start with some basic guidelines. Will you purchase only games rated T and below? This is what I have done in the past, because it modeled the library's policy about lending R-rated movies to minors. Talk to your teens. What kind of games do they want to play? Sports, racing, adventure? If you can only purchase a few games, then I recommend buying games with robust multiplayer modes, as these can be used in both programming, by solo players, and for circulation. This includes fighting games, racing games, sports games, and does not include (as much) adventure and war games—these can usually be played by more than one player but are not as much fun in groups. I would also make an effort to buy games that are of interest to as many teens as possible. Super-violent games will not appeal to all teens; singing games won't either. But if you can afford to get a well-rounded collection, get some of both. Think about your audience: girls and boys ages 12 to 19. There is a lot of variety there. What consoles will you be purchasing? The three biggies are the Nintendo Wii, the XBox 360, and the PlayStation 3.

Nintendo Wii

The Wii is extremely popular with people of all ages—and indeed it is the second-most popular of all the consoles—from children to adults, because of its revolutionary model of gameplay. The controllers, called Wii remotes (or wiimotes) are motion-sensitive and therefore respond to the movement of the player rather than the player pressing a certain combination of buttons on a controller. There are some Wii games that use the Wii remote in a more traditional way, but some of the most fun Wii games require whole-body movement, which is silly, exciting, and actually quite good exercise. In my experience, the Wii is very popular among younger teens, who are especially drawn to the *Wii Sports* package, a game that comes with every console. There are add-ons to the basic *Sports* package. Another fun one to get is *Wii Fit,* which comes with a platform that the player uses to stand, run, balance, or jump on. Wii games could be used in a fun multigenerational program; you might use *Wii Yoga* for a spa day with moms and daughters, or pit teens against tweens with *Wii Sports.*

You will often see younger children teaching their parents and even grandparents how to play with a Wii. I also would tentatively argue that girls seem to like the Wii more than any other console, since it tends to be intuitive and less intimidating than other consoles. But please take that statement with a grain of salt, since there are many girls who love video games of all colors. A Wii console will run you about $200 without any add-ons and with two controllers; games are about $20 to $30. Many games for the Wii are made for Nintendo and therefore can only be found for the Wii, but there are some games that are manufactured for the Wii plus another platform, such as the game *Call of Duty.*

Microsoft Xbox 360

The 360 is the third most popular of the latest generation of gaming consoles, though anecdotally, I find it to be the most popular among teenage boys when given a choice between the PlayStation, Wii, and Xbox. It was introduced by Microsoft in 2005, as a follow up to 2001's Xbox. The 360 allows players to get online and play friends anywhere in the world, which has allowed for cool events like the previously mentioned National Gaming Day, which pits teams from different libraries against each other in real time. The Xbox 360 Arcade in considered the entry-level 360; it offers a smaller hard drive for a smaller price tag—$199. If you purchase an Xbox Arcade, you will need to spend money on additional controllers (it only comes with one) and more memory if necessary. The Xbox 360 Elite is priced at $299 and includes significantly more memory. Memory is important because it allows players to save their games. To go online, you will need to purchase an Xbox Live membership. It's also worth noting that Xbox games can be played on Xbox 360s, a nice feature that may expand your video game collection if you already have Xbox games or if anyone has donated theirs. You can stream Netflix movies on 360s, as well as download games, movie trailers, and TV shows using the built-in Windows Media Center.

Kinect was released by Microsoft in November 2010. This is an add-on for Xbox 360s that allow for a controller-free gaming experience. Like the Wii, which uses controllers that respond to the player's movements and positions, Kinect senses the motions of the player—without a controller.

Players may use gestures or speech to control the game. Within ten days of its launch, one million units had been sold. Games for the console include *Dance Central, Def Jam Rapstar, Harry Potter and the Deathly Hallows: Part 1,* and *Zumba Fitness.* The XBOX add-on costs about $120 (you will already need the Xbox console); games start around $50.

Sony PlayStation 3

Sony's PlayStation franchise is the best-selling of all gaming consoles. 150 million PlayStation 2s have been sold since the PS2 was released in 2000, followed by 102.49 million PlayStations, the original console that was introduced in 1994. That said, the PS3, which came out in 2006, is the least popular of the big three, having sold 47.9 million units since it was introduced in 2006. The PS3 costs about $229 for a baseline, 40 GB model, and climbs to $450 for a 160 GB system, the largest currently available (a 250 GB model is in development as I write this). As with all the other consoles, there are some games that are exclusive to the PS3 and others that are manufactured for different systems. The PS3 offers an online gaming experience, called the PlayStation Network. Additionally, BluRay discs can be played on the PS3, a nice feature if you show movies in the teen area. If you have an HD hookup for your television, the images on PS3 games are crisp and gorgeous, and they look great with regular hookups, too.

Add-Ons

Some games need more equipment than others. The most extensive is *Rock Band,* which requires, for a complete experience, a drum set, microphone, and guitar. Two guitars mean that four people can play in all, with one singing and one playing the drums. *Guitar Hero* requires at least two guitars for teens to compete against each other. *DJ Hero* requires a turntable. Many Wii games need extra equipment, like *Wii Yoga* and *Wii Fit.* You can purchase steering wheels for *Mario Kart* that the Wii remotes fit into. *Dance Dance Revolution,* which admittedly appears to be out of fashion, comes with a huge mat that teens must dance on in order to win points. You will need as many controllers as you can afford (for a maximum of four), plus SD cards if you need extra memory. If your teens will be going online, they might need headsets so that they can talk to players in other places, and you'll need to pay for online access on a monthly basis if you want games to be live. Keep all of this in mind as you build your gaming budget and decide which console you want to purchase.

Handhelds

Some libraries purchase handheld games for teens so that they can play games while others are playing on the big screen, or to take home. Some of the most popular are the Nintendo DS, Nintendo's Game Boy Advanced, and the PlayStation Portable (or PSP). These handhelds require special games. Handhelds vary in price from $130 for the DS to $200 for a PSP. Games for handhelds can run from $15 to $30.

Computer Games

Planning a computer game collection can be a challenge because of the huge number of games available, and because of the difficulty of managing games. Computer games can either be purchased on CD-ROM, which means that the CD must be in the computer for the player to play, or downloaded. The cost of a game can be anywhere from $40 to $5 to free. And this does not take into account the thousands of games available to play online. How do you collect those? Should you even trouble yourself with them?

Mac games can be downloaded (for a fee) or purchased on CD-ROM. There are far fewer games for Macs than for PCs, and many serious gamers will tell you that Windows-based computers are better gaming machines, partly because more graphics hardware is available for Windows than Mac operating systems. Since most games are developed for Windows first, with the Mac as almost an afterthought, it can sometimes be difficult to find popular games for the Mac. If you are downloading games from a vendor site, you will find far more for Windows than for the Mac OS, and game management programs like Steam and GameTap are only available for Windows, too. However, Apple does have a game download site (http://www.apple.com/games/) and there are a few games that are either Mac-only or offered for the Mac that are wildly popular. They include:

The Sims. This huge franchise (currently up to *The Sims 3* with dozens of expansion packs) is popular with those who enjoy simulation games. It is a single-player-only game and would be hard to use in a library, as it does not offer the ability for multiple users to create profiles—rather, each player would be playing with a different Sims family in the same game. No one wins *The Sims*—it's one of those games that lasts forever and has infinite possibilities. However, there are certain tasks and goals that can be achieved in order to win rewards.

World of Warcraft. Known as *WoW*, this is the finest example around of a MMORPG—a Massively Multiplayer Online Role-Playing Game. Like *The Sims,* this game is one in a series—in this case, the *Warcraft* series. This, the most recent, was released in 2004. *WoW* would work better for libraries, as each player has an avatar that they control. Some libraries set up multiple computers so that players can all play *WoW* at the same time. Also like *The Sims,* there is no end to *WoW,* but players can undergo quests, the completion of which rewards the player with points, new skills, or money to use in the game.

Spore was released in 2008 with a huge amount of fanfare, as a result of its creature creator, a component of the game that allows players to custom-build characters that adapt and evolve throughout the course of the game. Players can also create content for the game and then make it available to other players to download and use in their own games. While professional reviews of the game were largely positive, some players and reviewers were frustrated with the short, too-simple first four levels; the space level (the fifth) is by far the most complex and interesting. But by far the most divisive issue was the digital rights management (DRM) built into every game: a player may only load Spore onto three computers, an issue that many find frustrating and unnecessary since the game retails for about $40.

Plants vs. Zombies. Like the other games above, PvZ is available for both Windows and Mac systems, but I have seen it played far more on Macs. This highly addictive 2009 release is simple in its concept—the player places plants in a yard to defend a house against a zombie attack. Different plants are made available in each level. Teens *love* this game; it's funny, challenging, and easy to learn.

Windows games are far too numerous to list in totality. The types of games available runs the gamut from adventure to first-person shooter to RPGs to simulation games…and beyond. In order to best purchase Windows games for your teens, I recommend asking them what they would like. Among the top-selling Windows games on Amazon.com as of March 2011, here are the top-five rated T or below:

- *Dragon Age 2.* A single-player role-playing game; with customizable characters and a large world to explore.
- *The Sims Medieval.* The gameplay of The Sims blended with Role Playing Game (RPG) elements; this is a new direction for the franchise.

- *Total War: Shogun 2.* A turn-based strategy game wherein the player assumes the identity of the leader of a warring province in Medieval Japan.
- *Starcraft II: Wings of Liberty.* Both single- and multiple-player campaigns are available; a real-time sci-fi strategy game.
- *LEGO Star Wars III: The Clone Wars.* An action-adventure game that can be played by single or multiple players.

In order to best make Windows games available to your teens, you will need to create gaming PCs for them. These are souped-up machines that allow for the highest-quality gameplay you can afford. In order to build a gaming PC, you will need to add a few things to an out-of-the-box computer:

- A videocard/graphics card. This piece of hardware will generate better images than what comes standard by accelerating the graphics output of the game and increasing the PC's video memory. In order to install one, you will need to remove the old graphics card and then follow the instructions that came with the new one very carefully—or hand it over to your IT manager, if you have one and he or she is willing to help. There are some useful videos on YouTube that show you exactly how they are installed if you want to take it on yourself.
- Extra memory (RAM). Giving your computer extra RAM boosts its performance because it allows the machine to multitask better—running multiple processes at once—and makes your computer capable of handling higher-quality graphics. To install more RAM, you can purchase RAM modules that snap into the motherboard. Again, I would ask someone in IT to give you a hand.
- Think about purchasing an out-of-the-box gaming PC. They may be more expensive, but you will not have to do any of the installation yourself. Most major PC manufacturers offer this as an option.

Managing Your Computer Game Collection

Making computer games available to your teens is not as easy as turning on the computer. You buy games on CD-ROM. The program files from that CD must be installed and then, usually, the CD needs to be in the drive in order to play the game. This can be a cumbersome process if you have many games and do not wish to constantly be switching out CDs. Instead, you might install one of many available content delivery programs.

Steam was created by Valve Corporation and is available at http://store. steampowered.com/. The Steam client is a free download; the games cost money, starting under $5. Steam offers about 1,100 games from most major game manufacturers. About 25 million people use Steam to manage their games, which are purchased through Steam, downloaded, and stored on the computer. The user creates a username and password to access the client. In the case of a library, you would probably want to log into Steam every morning and log off every evening. That way, teens could freely play games and you would not have to give out the login information.

GameTap is a similar program, this one created by the Turner Broadcasting System. GameTap works off a different model than Steam, though; users subscribe to the service by paying a monthly or annual fee and have access to game downloads.

Programming for Computer Gamers

Apart from video game programs, there are a few things you can do with computer games to make gaming a social experience.

LAN parties may seem like a throwback, but they are still happening and still popular with gamers. A LAN (Local Area Network) party involves getting a bunch of computers networked together so that teens can play each other right in the same room. Pizza and high-caffeine drinks are mandatory. For practical tips on how to manage a LAN party, take this *School Library Journal* article to your IT department: http://www.schoollibraryjournal. com/article/CA6640444.html.

Games Are Not Just Video Games

Teens like board games, too, and card games. In two libraries, I have found that teens love to play the board games of their childhood. Life, Guess Who, Connect 4, and Clue are all popular. Making available some decks of regular playing cards and other card games—Magic: The Gathering, Pokemon, and others—is also a good idea, though you may want to ask around to see whether teens are interested in such things before making too many purchases. Running monthly chess, checkers, Monopoly, or Scrabble tournaments can be an easy way to get teens together and teach them new skills. One of my staff members created a twice-monthly chess program that grew steadily in attendance and became a destination for teens who found it a challenging, fun way to spend an hour. He taught them new strategies and would play against teens who didn't have a partner.

Board games are nice to have lying around. Keep a collection out for teens to play whenever they want to take a break from homework, reading, or video games. You'll want to make sure they pick up after themselves, or else you'll lose pieces like crazy. If you can set up a table with the games on it, all the better—make that space a designated gaming area. You may find that word of mouth will spread and that teens start making a point of regularly stopping in for their checkers match.

Game Theft

For some reason, more than any other materials, librarians are worried about video game theft. Other items are just as easy to steal, but I think the perception is that video games are more desirable than any other material and therefore more likely to walk out the door. To this I say: build money into your budget for replacements. Like anything else, certain games will walk. It's frustrating because you have far fewer games than you do books, so the theft of one item can often mean that your collection is reduced by 20 percent. I do not think that the solution to game theft is to keep games hidden, locked away, or behind a desk. This limits their access, and games should not be treated in a way that books would not be treated. At the very least, start by keeping your games out. If you are in the teen lounge when teens are there, then you can at least keep an eye on things and prevent theft whenever possible. If they do disappear alarmingly fast, start taking them out of the room when you're not there.

Tech-Based Programs

While incorporating technology isn't always the golden ticket we hope it will be to reach teens, increasing numbers of teens are becoming interested in technology, either learning new skills or playing around with the ones they already have. Don't fall into the trap that so many adults do, which is that teens are fantastic with using technology and use it at every opportunity. My experience is that teens don't notice technology—it's constant and ever-present in their lives, which means they don't think anything of it—and there is a lot that they don't know. Yes, they can do anything with a cell phone, and yes, they're better at teaching themselves how to use new tech, but that doesn't mean that they're all great at using Word, doing research online, editing digital photos, or whatever skill it is that adults are always trying to learn.

- Make Your Own Computer Games. The best-known (and simplest) tool out there for designing computer games is Scratch, a program built by MIT and accessible at scratch.mit.edu. New users aren't going to be able to build the next big game, but they are going to learn about the basics of design and maybe even end up with a simple, playable, short game. You've got to spend some time playing around with Scratch on your own before teaching it; there are some good resources on the website, at http://info.scratch.mit. edu/Educators

- Teen Technology Tutors. Teens might not all be tech wunderkinds, but many of them do have technology skills that people of other generations do not. If there are seniors in your community who would like to learn very basic computer skills—like how to use a mouse, how to set up an e-mail account, how to buy airline tickets online—then teens could be the perfect people to teach them. These tutoring sessions could take place in scheduled one-on-one sessions or during set drop-in times. Teens can earn community service hours and at the end of each lesson, they'll feel really proud of themselves.

- Technology Advisory Board. Teen Advisory Boards are old hat, but what about a group that advises librarians on technology purchases, services, and programs? Keeping track of all the new tech coming down the pike is hard, so leave it up to the teens themselves to guide you. Make this a two-way program by asking your teens to test out new tech initiatives at your library, like text reference services, the new e-reader you bought for your reference collection, or downloadable audio books.

- Video editing. I've found that there is little that some teens like more than filming themselves doing just about anything. Buy a couple of Flip cameras (or similar types) and make them available just to teens. Once they've made their movie—lip-synching to Miley Cyrus songs, interviewing their friends, or putting on little skits—show them how to load the film into iMovie or another movie editor and edit it, add titles and effects, and then post it to the library's website.

- Weave tech into your traditional programs. Book groups can make book trailers using Animoto, a video slideshow maker with music. Writing groups can start a blog. Craft groups can take digital photos of their creations and post them online. Book discussions can become virtual on Facebook. Scavenger hunts become digital photo scavenger hunts.

- Podcasting. With a moderate amount of effort, you can produce a monthly podcast that's wholly written, recorded, and edited by teens. At the beginning, you will find you are doing much of the work, but with time and practice, the teen participants will begin taking the reins. Podcasts can be about anything. One formula is to create a monthly preview of teen programs and a discussion of the latest and hottest books, movies, and video games.
- Animating. The following downloads are fun, free and easy animation software programs:
  - Pivot Stickfigure Animator: http://pivot-stickfigure-animator.en.softonic.com/
  - Pencil: http://www.pencil-animation.org/
- Music making. Learn how to use the Garage Band music software program or bring in someone who can *really* show teens how it's done. ImaginOn at the Public Library of Charlotte and Mecklenberg County does amazing things with music making, like hooking up mics, keyboards, and other instruments to a computer and then letting teens remix their original creations. Visit their website (http://www.imaginon.org/Programs_&_Events/default.asp#tech) to find out more about what they do. Garage Band comes installed on Macs equipped with newer versions of Apple's iLife software bundle. Some music software for Windows systems:
  - Music Maker, $60
  - ACID Music Studio, $70
  - Cakewalk Music Creator 5, $40

Traditional Programs

Traditional programs are the bread and butter of teen programming. What's a teen department without craft activities, taste tests, and contests? What I've observed is that these programs tend to attract younger teens, although being in the right place at the right time can sometimes mean that high schoolers are diving into the activity with relish. Creative programming can get costly if you're buying supplies every week; some of these ideas require one-time (kinda expensive) purchases that can be used over and over again.

- Art. There are tons of ways to give teens an artistic outlet. Graphic novel workshops, when taught by cartoonists or graphic artists, can be a fantastic all-day program during the summer. Display teen art in your library or scan it and put it on your library's website. Ask teens to design art for *everything*—logos for publicity, posters, t-shirts, booklets, you name it.

- Crafts. Here's a brief list of craft activities that are easy to pull off:
  - T-shirt making. *Do this on newspaper. I can't stress this enough.* What you need: plain undershirts, fabric paint, ribbon, fabric glue. No iron-ons needed!
  - Cards for any occasion. What you need: cardstock, markers, stickers, stamps, glitter glue. Even better: make them for veterans, hospital patients, soldiers, or any other group that would love a cheery note.
  - Magnets. What you need: clear stones, pictures cut out from magazines, glue, and magnet backings.
  - Origami. What you need: origami paper, someone who knows how to make paper cranes.
  - Decorate candle holders, picture frames, you name it. What you need: paint markers, stickers, stamps, ribbon, glue, glitter, and unfinished products from craft stores. Glass markers plus any glass object (vases, tea light holders, etc.) are great.
  - Beading and jewelry making. What you need: jewelry wire, beads, earring backs, clasps, and the like. A neat project might be using junk to make jewelry, like keys from a computer keyboard, bottle caps, old keys, and so forth.
  - The craft "free-for-all." One of my favorite programs. What you need: *All* of your craft supplies in a plastic bin. Bring it into the teen area at a busy time, plop your bin down on the table, stand back, and watch the magic happen.
- Food, food, food. Cookie decorating and dessert bake-offs satisfy the sweet tooth, and local restaurant taste-offs bring the big eaters. Try pizza—just make sure you cut up the pieces into smaller bites, or else you'll be ordering dozens of pizzas and nursing some stomach aches. Got a lot of bakeries in town? Cupcakes or cookies can be another taste test. Many librarians do "gross out" contests, à la *Fear Factor,* but I've never been brave enough to try it. Serve pie on Pi Day (the March 14 holiday in honor of the mathematical constant). Blind taste tests could be funny…just avoid anything with nuts. And did you know there's a National Potato Chip Day?
- Contests. It's true—teens love to win things, whether it's big (a PS3 for one Summer Reading finale party raffle prize drew

record crowds) or small (candy), teens want it for themselves. Some easy contests to run:

- Sappiest poem contest in February. The cheesier the better.
- Scavenger hunts. Get the rest of the staff in on the fun and put a clue at every service desk.
- Guessing games. How many books are there in the library? How many years has the library been open? What three teen books have the most names on their waiting lists right now?
- Spelling bees. Can be done at the drop at the hat. Bring your Webster's.
- Raffles. Come to an event and enter your name in the prize drawing. Easy!

Family and Multigenerational Programs

Teen programs don't always have to be just for teens. As the teen librarian, it's also your responsibility to reach out to parents and families of teens. This can mean younger siblings or grandparents. Certain programs lend themselves better to all-ages attendance. If you are holding a contest and planning an awards ceremony, invite families. It's a great way to involve parents and siblings in a library event and build pride in teens and in the library. Some larger-scale programs also might be fun for parents to attend, like talent competitions or concerts. Just think carefully about what you want the atmosphere of the program to be. Once adults can attend, the program will change. Not necessarily for the worse, but it will change. If you want teens to feel as comfortable as possible being themselves, then leave it teen-only. If you think that teens will benefit from having their families there to cheer them on, then open it up. You could always invite parents to one in a series of programs, but again, think carefully about this. In general, teen programs should be teen-only.

Multigenerational programs, family or not, can be an excellent addition to an events calendar. These are planned specifically to be multigenerational and all involved know going in that patrons of all ages will be attending. These programs are multigenerational by design rather than arbitrarily. Some examples of programs that would work for teens and older patrons:

- Storytelling. Teens interview (and video) adults telling stories about their community or their childhood. Teens then edit the videos, which are kept as an oral history on the library website.

- Mother/daughter or father/son activities. Book groups and workshops can be a nice setting for parents to do an activity with their child(ren). This does not have to be gender-specific, though it can help guide you in planning something appealing. Another idea is to run field trips to museums, author readings, or publishing conventions with teens and their parents.

- Grandparent gaming. Wii games can be popular with seniors due to their capacity to encourage low-impact exercise. Teens can bowl against their grandparents or play them in a tennis match. A program similar to this was developed by the Darien Library children's library for children and their grandparents, and it could work just as well with teens.

Teens can also be in programs with younger children:

- Scratch classes. Scratch, which is described earlier in this chapter, would lend itself well to a multigenerational program due to its appeal to children and teens of varied ages. Teens can teach children, either paired one-on-one or circulating among a larger group of children. The class should have a goal at its core; that is, a project that everyone can work on at the same time. This format can be applied to any kind of technology class.

- Volunteering in the children's library. If your children's library has this opportunity available, set up teens with groups of children to read them stories, help with craft programs, chaperone big events, or act as a second pair of hands during story times.

- Tween/teen socials. This works when teens and children are a bit closer in age—upper elementary school kids with middle schoolers, for example. You might develop a program that will make tweens feel more comfortable making the transition from the children's library to the teen lounge. This could involve a cupcake social, an open meeting of the Teen Advisory Board that older children can attend, or a mentoring program that pairs TAB members with active children's library users.

- Homework help. Have teens volunteer to staff drop-in homework sessions after school, where younger students (this would work best for upper elementary or younger middle schoolers) can get extra help with their assignments.

Academic

Whether or not teens in your community are, as a whole, high-achieving and college bound, there will always be a group who are interested in getting more information about college, as well as tools to help them better navigate the maze of high school academics. As you get to know what teens in your community are interested in, school-wise, you will be able to plan events that help make them better students. School and public librarians should keep in close contact throughout this process, both to avoid repeating already-existing programs and for public librarians to have the most information possible about what the schools can offer and what the needs of the teens are. Some ideas:

- *Library instruction.* This is usually the domain of the school librarian, but school librarians can't always do all the instruction they want, and even if they can, there's no reason not to reinforce it at the public library. These sessions might be targeted to specific databases or websites that the school library doesn't offer. You could do MLA and other citation style refreshers. You could offer a mini-class on website evaluation. You could even run writing lab workshops, staffed either by you or by students, on a regular basis. Teens could bring their writing and have it peer edited. Or teach classes on certain computer programs that are often required by teachers, like PowerPoint.

- *Study support.* Reserve study rooms during busy after-school times for teens to use. Invite teachers to use library space for extra help sessions. Make certain areas quiet areas during heavy study times. Staff the reference area with a teen librarian during finals for more support. Stay open late during midterms and finals for teens who need to study hard. Let teens bring food into the library so that they can feed their brains during testing weeks. Offer snack breaks, yoga breaks, board game breaks. Bring in power strips so that more teens can charge their laptops. Make sure you let the schools know if you are doing any of this so that they can promote it to the students themselves.

- *College admissions.* Be careful about inviting in representatives from companies to run these programs, as your library may not allow for-profit organizations to promote their services. Kaplan and other agencies are eager to teach classes on college essays, SAT prep, and so forth. If that's not a possibility, find local professionals who can teach classes, such as teachers, guidance counselors, or local authors. If there is an adult education center in your community, you may be able to find instructors who will teach a college essay class for free or for cheap. Check, too, at the local community college. One program that worked well for me was a panel discussion of college admissions issues. I organized two programs, one with general admissions info and one with information for student athletes. The people who sat on the panel were parents, teachers, coaches, admissions counselors, guidance counselors, and students. The events were for parents and teens, something I recommend, as parents can often be heavily involved in the admissions process.

SUMMER READING

Summer reading programming is sometimes the only big programming season in public libraries. In others, it might not be the only one, but it's still the biggest. Even if librarians don't want to spend tons of time and money on summer reading programs, it's hard to avoid. The public expects it. And, it's a wonderful time to promote library services and get teens into the library. I often saw teens during the summer that I never saw throughout the school year. (And conversely, some school year regulars will disappear during the summer.) The summer is a different time from the rest of the year—programming times can become more flexible, kids get up later, and the weekends might be empty. Try to get a sense of usage patterns, if you can, but if you don't have time to do your research, consider holding programs in the afternoon, Tuesday through Thursday; many families go away on the weekends during the summer. Keep notes so that you will be able to learn from your experiences every year.

Promoting

The number one rule for getting the word out about summer reading is: get into the schools. Speak with your friends at your local middle and high school libraries and see if you can schedule a time in late spring/early summer to speak with the students about summer reading. It's easier to do this if you're doing something else, too, like bringing in summer reading suggestions and doing booktalks. Or, it might be easier just to pop into as many classrooms as you can to hand out flyers and verbalize the highlights. Print out calendars that can be stuck to refrigerators, and create bright, eye-catching flyers with major programs and prize-winning opportunities, plus any details about how to sign up.

Work with local businesses to not only co-sponsor events and prizes but also to advertise. Put up flyers in the local summer haunts—coffee shops, pizza places, delis. Since your chance to advertise through the schools goes away at the end of classes, you'll need to find another way to reach out to parents and teens. If you've been collecting e-mail addresses at programs, consolidate them and send out a weekly highlight e-mail (make sure you offer the opportunity to opt out of the e-mails). Press releases to the local papers will help because parents will be looking for things for their kids to do. The same goes for local blogs and online events calendars. And make sure your flyers and calendars are *all* over the library.

Partnering

You can develop a great summer reading lineup on your own, but things really get interesting when you bring in outsiders. They lend an air of authority to certain events and make others special because they're different from the norm. Be sure to reach out to people far in advance, as summer dates book up fast, and keep in mind that you'll need ample time to plan and promote. Here are a few ideas to get started:

- Instructors and teachers:
  - Arts centers may be able to lend their teachers for a free class if they are allowed to leave out a copy of their own class schedule.
  - Schoolteachers could lead workshops—on technology, cooking, creative writing, robotics, computer programming, and the like. They may ask for a small fee.
  - Businesses like yoga studios, sports camps, gyms, or spas might be willing to come in for a sports clinic, spa day, yoga class, or fitness class.
  - Local writers, artists, filmmakers, actors, and other private citizens could happily share their knowledge with teens in a workshop.
  - Social services employees, those who work in the schools or other agencies, might be interested in coming in to lead a discussion group, either for parents or teens themselves. Chances are, this would be gratis.
- Local businesses:
  - If you're doing taste tests, ask pizza places, bakeries, or grocery stores to donate the goods. The winning vendors might even advertise the accolade in their store.
  - Ask stores to donate prizes—gift cards are always a good idea.
  - Stores might also donate refreshments, if you credit them for doing so.

- Bookstores might donate multiple copies of books, or sell their own copies to teens, if you're hosting an author visit.
- Getting off-site:
  - Ask the parks department, the schools, the town hall, anyone, if you can hold library programs in their space. A music program might work in the town amphitheatre, or you could have a skateboarding clinic in the parking lot of the high school. Yoga could be held in the park, or a photography class might take a field trip to a local attraction.
  - See if you can hold events at local businesses. How cool would it be to have an open mic night at a real coffeehouse?
  - Take your teens to do community service at local organizations, or on field trips to learn. Trips to plays, concerts, recitals, or readings could be a highly enriching experience. Just make sure you call ahead instead of just dropping by.

Summer Programs

Summer allows for a wide variety of programming, perhaps more than during the rest of the year. It's a nice chance to try things out that you can't during the year due to time constraints and teens who are pulled in too many directions. Here are some ideas for fun, special programs that work well in the summer:

- Mini camps. Run a week-long tech camp, writing camp, or acting camp. I recommend making the days short and serving lunch or snacks. Also, make this a registered event, especially if you're hiring outside instructors.
- Late-night events. If your library is open late—or even if it isn't—the summer is an opportunity for you to hold evening events. The kids don't have to get up early! See if you can keep the place open late if you normally close early. Concerts, movies, and improv groups are all excellent events to hold late at night.
- Outdoor activities. Head outside for water balloon fights, tie dyeing, soccer clinics, mural painting, picnics, or scavenger hunts.

In addition to all this, make sure you start and end summer with a bang. Have a kick-off party and a finale party. These can be any big event—a dance party, a huge video game tournament, or a battle of the bands—or just a celebration with pizza, prizes, and music.

Prizes

Prizes can be key to participation in summer reading, especially in new programs. Not so much bribes, prizes are ways of attracting teens' attention. They also show that you mean business; you're not just throwing together any old program for them, you're actually spending time and money on them. There are a few ways to give away prizes during summer reading, or any program or series of programs, for that matter.

- Ask teens to review what they're reading, listening to, and watching. Every time they turn in a review, they get a ticket for a raffle. If you're getting tons of entries, this could be a weekly raffle, or if things are slower, you could hold one big prize drawing at the end of the summer. Or, in combination, you could enter all of the reviewers in both: once for the weekly drawing during the week they enter, and then again at the end of the summer.
- At big events, hand out tickets for door prizes. Make sure you advertise what you're giving away, especially if it's a big-ticket item.
- Hold contests that are fun for summer—summer-themed photo contests, outdoor scavenger hunts, or pie-eating competitions.

Teen Involvement

It's especially fun to get teens involved in summer reading, and there are a few ways to do so.

- Develop a summer-only volunteer program, with special jobs just for teens, like helping set up for events, putting handwritten book reviews online, or decorating the teen area to make it more summery. See if they can help with children's summer reading events—ask the head children's librarian.
- Ask your teen advisory board to plan one or two of the programs over the summer, too. They may have some valuable ideas.
- Get teens writing reviews. You can either have paper forms for them to fill out by hand—a bookmark-sized slip of paper is the easiest way to do this; you can just stick it into a book when they check it out—or create an online form that will allow for reviews to be posted on your website. Or, ask teens to write them on paper cut out in different shapes and then displayed in the teen area. This might sound childish, but teens love it—having their work

on display can be a big thrill. Reviews don't just have to be for books, either—make sure they know they can review movies, games, music, TV shows, and so on.

Summer Reading Lists

If you are in communication with the schools, then it's important to find out if the schools have a required reading list for their students, or a list of books that students have to choose from over the summer. You will want to make sure to have these books on hand. If you can afford it, try to get more than one copy. Students will come in looking for these titles over the summer, and it's a shame if there aren't enough copies to go around, as that means some teens may never have the chance to read the book before school starts up again in the fall. If you can, start these conversations with the schools early, and let them know what your limitations are. If you have any influence at all, you might suggest that they not have a required or even suggested reading list, but allow for free choice—perhaps with the criterion that the teen needs to show that the book is reviewed or that it was recommended by a librarian. A modified version of this is to offer a longer list, asking teens to select a certain number of books on it (three to five is usually about right). If the schools see that your budgetary restrictions don't allow you to purchase more than one or two copies of each title, they may see the point, which is that by requiring that certain books be read, they are essentially asking their students to purchase these items.

If the schools in your community do not publish a required reading list, then you will want to create book lists to have on hand for when teens come in during the summer. Teens will generally need to read a book either for school, or because their parents are making them, or because they want to. Teens who are not voracious readers might not know where to begin to look. Themed booklists are easy to create and can be made to look catchy fairly easily. Create lists of about twenty books, with cover images if possible, and brief annotations. Give the lists fun names, laminate them, and hang them up in the room. Or, print out a ton of copies and leave them lying around. Or, put them online so that teens can print them out. You might also consider increasing the number of displays you have in the area during the summer, as teens like to grab and go on their way to a family vacation or to the pool.

COMMUNITY PROGRAMMING

As I have mentioned previously, before you start working with other community organizations on programming, chat with your director about any restrictions the library might have on outside groups conducting programs in the library. For example, some libraries do not allow groups that fundraise or promote their services. This can be tricky when you are working with groups like test prep companies that would like to put their logo on their materials and make a pitch for their services. In some libraries, policies prohibit this. It's also just a good idea to get a sense of which groups have worked with the library in the past and whether there is any history between the library and other organizations. During this conversation, your director may give you the names of already-existing contacts in certain organizations, which is a great place to start. There's no need to reinvent the wheel.

Once you're clear on the parameters of how you might work with other organizations, start thinking about what kind of programs you might want to collaborate on. Presumably, you're not an expert on absolutely everything, so what have the teens been asking for—or what have you wanted to try—that you haven't been able to provide on your own? Maybe it's music classes, or a breakdance competition, or a graphic novel workshop. In other words, what gaps are there in the library's programming for teens that you would like to fill?

Next, it's time to see what resources exist in your community. This might include arts centers, community theaters, municipal sports teams, or social services groups. The possibilities for collaboration are endless. You might even co-sponsor a program, which means that both organizations take financial responsibility for the program and both work to promote it. In this case, both the library and the outside group's name would go on all publicity. Alternatively, you might hire or ask someone to volunteer to come in to teach a class. This would probably be a library-only program, but you may want to advertise the instructor's affiliation, since that could be a draw. An outside group could also provide an expert to lead a discussion group or give a talk. This could be a college admissions program, a discussion of relevant issues, or a lecture on Internet safety.

Even if you don't have any specific ideas for a collaborative program, take some time to introduce yourself to the leaders of different organizations in town. You will want to let them know that you are open to co-sponsoring programs and that they should definitely contact you if they have any ideas of their own. The nice thing about working with already-established community organizations is that they already have an audience. If your library has superior facilities, perhaps someone would consider holding one of their own events in the library—a yoga class, for example, or an improv workshop. If these events are part of a series, then the library will benefit from a built-in audience, and the community organization will expand their programs to a different group. It's a win-win.

WHAT TO DO WHEN NO ONE COMES

I promise you that there will be times when not a single person comes to your program. I promise that it will happen more than once. If it doesn't, then could you please get in touch with me and let me know what you're doing? The thing about teens is that they're not predictable. We can try to anticipate what they'll be interested in, and we might even hear dozens of teens tell us that such-and-such is a great idea, and then, when it comes time for them to put their money where their mouth is, the room remains empty. What happened? Did you mess up somehow? Chances are: no. There are many factors that could have contributed to the nonexistent turnout.

Schedule conflict. Teens in all communities are pulled in a million different directions, whether it's a plethora of extracurricular activities, after-school jobs, babysitting duties, homework, sports, or social activities. Don't think that you will ever be able to anticipate every potential conflict, but there are a couple of places you can look before you put stuff on the calendar. The school system may post an events calendar on their website. Be sure to check athletic contest calendars, too. Local papers often post events, though they tend to be only a week or two in advance. For a super big program that you really don't want to have compete with another event, call your contacts at the schools. They will have the best sense of what's happening in town. If there is a community calendar online anywhere, check it. The problem is that not everyone reciprocates this research—you might choose a date six months ahead that is free and clear, only to have another group schedule, just four weeks beforehand, an event on that identical date. That's life; there's nothing you can do about it except keep the channels of communication as open as possible between the library, the schools, and anyone else planning programs for teens.

It's worth mentioning in this section the fear I have heard about from other librarians of stepping on the toes of already-existing organizations. This is inevitable. If the library has until now not been programming for teens, then other groups have been filling that void and have been unaccustomed to competition. But first of all, there are going to be topics that are not covered by other groups already, and second of all, it's OK to compete a little. You may consider co-sponsorship before out-and-out competition, but you also have the right to run the programs you want to run. Just keep in mind that programs that have already been around for a while may beat you out when it comes to drawing an audience. That caveat aside, there are always topics that can't be done enough, and anything can be modified enough to make it special and unique to the library. Continue talking to people to avoid animosity developing—this may just be an issue in small towns—but do feel confident to create the programs you want, regardless of who might feel threatened.

Publicity missteps. It will take a little while before you have a good formula down for publicity. See Chapter 6 for specific tips on how to best publicize your program. In the meantime, some basic pitfalls: publicizing only on your library website; not publicizing enough; publicizing too early or too late; targeting teens and ignoring parents; not enlisting in teen help. When no one comes, it's a chance to think about how you publicized the program and where you might have gone wrong or not done enough. Sometimes it feels like you're going overboard, saturating the market with one program and driving people crazy, but trust me: you're not. Sometimes people need to see something five times to really *see* it, and the more people see something, the more likely they are to know that it's important.

Timing. Certain times of the year are better than others for teens. The beginning of the school year is always insane. The end of the school year is like a free-for-all. The holidays are distracting. And during the week, some days and times are better than others. When is the room the busiest from everyday use? When do teens go home at the end of the day? On the weekends, teens have sporting events and family obligations. It's not possible to keep track of all of these commitments and restrictions, and you shouldn't hold yourself responsible for messing up the timing of a program. However, there are a few things you can do to stack the deck in your favor:

- Track the busiest times in the library. Keep a head count of who's in the teen area or how many teens are in the rest of the library at different times: after school, in the evenings, and on the weekends. Do this for a week or even longer if you can.

- Find out what else is going on in town. Check the school calendars, the athletic schedules, and the local community calendars.
- Keep statistics at your programs. Count the number of teens who show up and note the time and day of the week.

It's just the wrong program. It's possible that the program you planned just isn't the right one. I am an advocate of creating programs for the audience you have, at least in the beginning. Take the time to build your audience before you take major risks in planning programs. Fill the needs that are already there and let the teens guide you. At the risk of sounding critical, I will say that in library school I had a certain picture in my head of what kinds of programs I would be planning for teens, and they all tended to be along the same lines: alternative, edgy programs for teens who weren't able to find appealing activities at mainstream venues. While that kind of program is certainly valuable and applicable in some libraries, I have found that the most successful programs are not based on my idea of what is cool, but, rather, on the teens' idea—and that is often pretty mainstream. But that is just my experience. Take the time to figure out what experience your teens want.

Don't trash a program just because it fails once. I have had many programs be unattended over and over again before the teens start to trickle in. Sometimes it just takes time for them to learn about it. All it takes is for one teen to show up, have fun, and then tell his or her friends about it.

BUDGET CONSTRAINTS

If you had all the money in the world, you could run hundreds of fabulous programs with expensive prizes and fancy refreshments. But you don't have all the money in the world—no teen librarian does. Even those in relatively wealthy libraries don't get everything they want come budget season. Just like with any other line item, you will have to be creative, find ways to save, and pick and choose your programs wisely. Try some of these programs on for size. They're either free or cheap, though they will require staff time—and as we know, time is money! Following this list is another list, this one of places where you can find cheap stuff, including inexpensive (or even free) prizes.

- Collage making. Take all of your discarded magazines and toss them in a giant heap. Provide card stock, Elmer's glue, markers, glitter, stickers, and anything else you can scrounge up. Teens can make gifts for their friends or art to decorate their lockers or bed-room walls.

- Dance competitions. All you have to do is make some room and put on some music. You can be the judge, or get other teens to score their peers based on a rubric.
- Mix CD swapping. Teens bring in CDs with their favorite songs and share with friends. You'll need a computer with a CD burner.
- Homework help. Snacks are great for a program like this, but if you can't swing it, just set up shop somewhere quiet and offer to help with math problems, et al.
- Worksheets/crossword puzzles/word games. Print out activities from sites like http://puzzlemaker.discoveryeducation.com/ or http://www.suntimes.com/lifestyles/crossword/index.html. Have races to see who can finish first.
- Scavenger hunts in the library. If you have access to a digital camera, make it a photo scavenger hunt where teens take photos of the clues. If not, just print out a worksheet and send them all over the library, making sure to require that they speak to different staff members! This can be a great opportunity to familiarize teens with areas of the library they might not normally visit.
- "(Your Town's Name) Idol." This can easily done with a version of the *American Idol* video game, but can also be done for free in a room where sound won't bother other patrons too much. I would suggest that you judge, since teens might not be especially tactful in their criticisms.
- Author visits. It may surprise you given the large fees some authors charge for visits, but these can be free. First of all, you can have teens speak with authors over Skype or speakerphone. Secondly, if you want an author to visit the building, many of them will do it gratis, especially if they're promoting a book. You will likely want to find authors who either live locally or are touring in the area, as some authors will ask for travel expenses if they're making a special trip. To see a list of authors in your area, visit YALSA's list of YA authors by state at http://wikis.ala.org/yalsa/index.php/ List_of_YA_Authors_by_State. And to learn how to coordinate an author visit via Skype, read this article in *School Library Journal:* http://www.schoollibraryjournal.com/article/CA6673572.html.
- Murder Mystery Night. Carleton College has an awesome how-to on library murder mystery games, which you can adapt to your own library, at http://www.carleton.edu/campus/library/ref erence/workshops/MurderMystery.html. A Google search for

library murder mystery will turn up loads of results, as this is an extremely popular event for people of all ages.

- Open Mic Night. Again, snacks would be lovely, and they can be cheap, but Open Mic Night is fun even without snacks. For this program, all you need is teens. They can bring their own instruments, voices, and writing. You will need to find a space in the library where other teens can gather to listen.

Inexpensive and Free Stuff

- Big box stores have good sales and deep discounts. Target, Walmart, Michael's, Kmart, and Party City are all places to start. Some of these stores offer discounts by e-mail if you sign up with them.
- School supply stores, both online and brick-and-mortar, also offer deals.
- Discount School Supply: http://www.discountschoolsupply.com.
- Lakeshore Learning: http://www.lakeshorelearning.com.
- Oriental Trading and Pearl River can be a great place for affordable prizes and decor. Visit http://www.orientaltrading.com or http://www.pearlriver.com.
- Use Zazzle for customized gifts (http://www.zazzle.com).
- The Library Store (http://www.thelibrarystore.com) has a section for clearance items at 50 percent off and more.
- You can always find sales on Amazon, and if you order enough, you'll get free shipping.
- Junk food always works as a prize. A giant bag of M & Ms will run less than $5 and be a huge hit. Another favorite is the "World's Largest Reese's Peanut Butter Cups," which cost about $10 and are 16 oz. of candy. They're a great novelty item and one that teens love to win (and try to prove they can eat in one sitting—they can't). Do be aware of nut allergies! It might be smart to have jelly beans or Twizzlers lying around as a backup.

Prizes need not be physical objects. Try these:

- Fine relief. Limit this in case a teen has lots and lots of fines—a $5 voucher should do it; this allows teens with no fines to save something for a rainy day.
- Special library privileges. Let a teen pick the video game being used for the upcoming tournament, or be "librarian for a day." If you have art in your teen room, let the winner put their creation

front and center. Put their photo in a prominent place on your website, or in the teen lounge with "WINNER" in big shiny letters under their picture.

- A library party. Teens can use a library space to have a party with their friends. Let them use the movie screen, your sound system, or your video games. Or, allow them to just bring their own food into an area that is usually food-free—that alone is a big deal.

ADVOCATING FOR TEEN PROGRAMMING

Programming for young adults may seem like a no-brainer, but sometimes it can make waves.

Gaming Programs

Gaming, which gets talked about so much among librarians that you might take it for granted, can still be a controversial issue for administrators, parents, and community members. Some might argue that games don't belong in libraries, which are for reading, studying, and doing research. The theory there is that gaming is less valuable than other library pursuits. Others might be uncomfortable with gaming because video games can sometimes feature violence or other potentially inappropriate content. In more traditional communities, or if your library has never provided gaming resources or programming before, it is a good idea to be prepared for criticism and even direct challenges. In fact, you may find yourself in the position of defending gaming to your library director or board of trustees. Be prepared. Go to your manager and propose that the library initiate a gaming program, and outline the reasons why gaming is both beneficial to teens and a positive service for the library to provide. Write down a defense of gaming to have at the ready if anyone ever calls it into question. And make sure that your library director is on board and knows what's going on.

I encourage you to not use the argument with naysayers that gaming gets teens into the library where they can be encouraged to read books. First of all, there's no telling that this strategy will work, and second of all, books are not inherently more valuable than games. Using games as a means to an end rather than acknowledging their intrinsic benefits is disingenuous and will do little to earn you the trust or respect of teens.

Below, I've outlined some talking points for you, as well as some resources that will provide you with the detail you need to fully advocate for gaming in libraries.

- Gaming in the library has social benefits. Teens come to the library, a common space, to play video games with friends and peers. They may spend time there with teens they don't know well, allowing them to meet new people and perhaps make new friends.

- If a library offers video games, then teens are more likely to frequent the library, which means that they are spending their unscheduled time in a place where they are safe.

- Gaming programs can lead to positive experiences with adults and other teens. Teens will see that adults value them enough to provide them with activities that teens will truly enjoy, and perhaps they will even interact with adults (librarians) in game play.

- Gaming can have a positive impact on literacy. All games require players to read. Video games use text in cut scenes to provide context, give written instructions on game play and missions, and sometimes require the player to choose options from text (such as in *Rock Band*, where players must choose a song from a list of titles).[1]

- Gaming promotes another kind of literacy—information literacy. Players must evaluate information and make choices in games based on the data they are presented with. This is the definition of critical thinking and problem solving.

For more talking points, read librarian Jack Martin's FAQ about gaming in libraries here: http://librarygamingtoolkit.org/faq.html. I especially appreciate that he asserts that libraries have a responsibility to "provide cultural, recreational, and entertaining materials, as well as informational and educational materials. Games provide stories and information as they entertain and educate." He also addresses different arguments against gaming, such as the assertion that gaming is fluff, addictive, and a distraction from books.

Stephanie Bedell wrote an excellent paper, which is published on the Internet Public Library, about how gaming supports social and education development. It can be found here: http://ipl.ci.fsu.edu/community/ wiki/index.php/Libraries_and_Gaming:_Supporting_Social_and_Edu cational_Development. Her paper and corresponding presentation (at http://prezi.com/bvc3ntia9ysr/gaming-the-library/) do an effective job of linking gaming to the 40 Developmental Assets, as well as the "new literacies." Be sure to browse through the resources she lists at the end of the article.

An article by Ameet Doshi in the May 2006 issue of Computers in Libraries gives a synopsis of the 2005 Gaming, Learning and Libraries symposium sponsored by the Metropolitan Library System in Chicago and then offers additional thoughts about gaming and literacy. The article can be found here: http://www.infotoday.com/cilmag/may06/Doshi.shtml. Doshi describes how gaming could be used by libraries specifically to promote information literacy. It is not so much a defense of gaming as it is an illustration of how gaming might be applied to literacy skill building.

Discussion Groups

If you lead any discussion groups on controversial topics, you may find that some parents are uncomfortable with this. If you are interested in hosting a regular gathering where teens can talk about issues affecting them, such as bullying, peer pressure, and even what's happening in the news, you might want to bring in an outside person to lead these discussions, someone who is professionally qualified.

Just as you might be thoughtful about the books that you recommend to teens or put on recommended reading lists, you might also need to be thoughtful about the books you select for book groups. It can sometimes help to create book groups that fall within specific age ranges, especially to separate teens in middle school from teens in high school. This will allow you to select books for these groups that are age appropriate.

Age Limits

If you set age limits on your teen programs, you might hear from parents who are frustrated that their children can't attend. You might also hear from tweens who want to go, or even adults who want to go. Have confidence that your decision to limit the ages of those who can attend teen programs is a good thing. The experiences of teens, children, and adults are different and those three groups have different needs. Additionally, you want the teens attending these programs to be comfortable. Having children or adults present might make them less so.

Make sure that age limits are posted on all of your publicity. Something like "this event is for teens aged 12 and up" can suffice. If it is a registered event, you can ask the age of the attendee. If not, you will just have to ask those who look like they may be too old or too young to be there, which can be awkward, but it's important. You will damage your credibility with teens if you allow anyone but teens to be at their events. Make sure your administration is on board with this.

NOTE

1. "The Librarian's Guide to Gaming: An Online Toolkit for Building Gaming @ Your Library," *Libraries, Literacy, and Gaming,* available at http://librarygaming toolkit.org/literacy.html.

5

$\diamond \ \diamond \ \diamond$

THE TEEN ADVISORY BOARD

The Teen Advisory Board, or TAB, is often the backbone of a teen program. In the beginning, these teens are your allies. They are your first core group of kids who will help you get your feet off the ground. Creating and maintaining a TAB might be essential to creating a successful program, and I definitely encourage you to make this one of your first priorities at a new job.

RECRUITING MEMBERS

Many librarians have asked me how to find teens to be on the advisory board. Well, to be honest, I got lucky at Darien Library. Because of the buzz surrounding the new library, I was able to offer tours before opening day to teens. It was a great way to get teens talking to their friends about the library and a way for us to get feedback from them about the new space. I contacted someone at our local teen center and she helped me round up a couple of tour groups. After the tours, I asked the teens if they wanted to sign up for the Teen Advisory Board. Many of them did, perhaps because of how great the new building looked. They wanted to be a part of it!

While you may not have a new library building to help you lure in teens, you do have a new teen program and a new teen librarian—you.

And just like I did, you can get people to help you connect with teens. The school librarian would be a perfect place to start, and then anyone else in the community who works with teens. Is there a volunteer group at the high school, or a job center that also advertises community service opportunities? Send them a brief synopsis of the TAB and its requirements and activities. I attended the high school's volunteer fair for two years and got lots of kids to sign up for volunteering at the library. They weren't all interested in joining the TAB, but many of them were. Other librarians have told me they've had great luck with simply putting table tents up near computers, teen or otherwise. And make sure you advertise on social networking sites like Facebook, and the library's website, of course. I created a simple, colorful logo for our TAB and used it in all of my publicity and on the TAB's Facebook page. It makes the group feel more cohesive and more like an institution, an established group.

Once you've got a group, no matter how small, ask them to recruit their friends. The goal, I think, is to a get a well-rounded group of kids: boys and girls, teens of different ages, and teens of different cliques and social circles. If one group is dominant—the theater kids, for example—then other teens might not feel comfortable participating. So reach out to different youth groups and advertise in a variety of places.

STRUCTURE

You may wish to create a smaller governing group within the TAB. Darien Library's had what we called an exec board, made up of some of the earliest joiners of the group. This included a president, vice president, secretary, treasurer, middle school representative, publicity manager, and event planner. We had so many on the exec board because so many teens were interested in taking leadership positions. And indeed, they were the teens who were most involved. I also went to them first with major questions, like about meeting changes, potential programs, or membership issues. I recommend holding elections every year; otherwise, an elected freshman might be in charge for four years, which is a long time and keeps other teens from having a chance at a leadership role.

It's wise to promote your TAB as a volunteer opportunity. Make sure you offer to sign off on community service hours and write recommendations. Teens deserve to get something back for giving their free time to the library. If there are any other perks you can offer them—after hours events, book previews, ARCs, fine leniency—do it. It will help you attract teens and also show your gratitude for their hard work. If you want to dole out rewards after a certain amount of activity in the group, that could prevent teens from joining just for the perks.

I also want to mention a thought that has often crossed my mind, which is that it may be worth considering having two TABs, one for older teens and one for younger. There are arguments against this, but some of the arguments for it are that older teens are often frustrated by the antics and immaturity of younger teens, and younger teens are often intimidated by older teens. I have dealt with some unproductive meetings as a result of older teens getting distracted by silly younger teens, who cannot focus on the task at hand. At the same time, younger teens have dropped out of the TAB because they do not feel like the older teens like or respect them. This could just be an issue of management by the adult in charge (in this case, me), but I also think that older and younger teens have different needs and expectations.

You can either be present at TAB meetings or let the teens have it all to themselves. The advantages of being there: you can instantly address their questions and concerns, or promise to find the answer for them. You can quell conflict or help keep the group focused. You can get to know the teens better. The advantages to not being there: the teens may feel like they can speak more freely. They can still bring issues and questions to you after the fact. The teens get to create their own agenda and have total ownership over TAB. The need to create order will help build responsibility and interpersonal skills. If you want, you could be present for most of the meeting and then leave to give them a chance to talk amongst themselves.

No matter what, make sure you serve food. Period.

RESPONSIBILITIES

You can do whatever you want with your TAB, as long as you keep in mind that, really, it belongs to the teens. It depends on what your goals are. If you want your TAB to be the voice of teens in your library, then the group becomes more of a *true* advisory board—they advise you on library issues. One member of the TAB might, for example, attend board meetings as a junior member. That teen would represent the opinions and interests of all teens using the library.

Other ways to give your TAB a voice:

- Have them come to an all-staff meeting to talk to your colleagues about their concerns or questions about the library

- Set up a quarterly meeting with a TAB representative and the library director
- Ask TAB members to volunteer at library events, like the book sale or fundraising events
- If your library has a friends group, form a "junior friends" group that asks teens to staff donation tables, run a bake sale, or design a mailer

If your TAB is about issues, then it could help to give the meetings some structure. You don't want to have each meeting be a free-for-all of complaints and ideas. With the president or another teen presiding, ask specific questions. If the library has begun circulating video games, which video games to they recommend you buy? If food is no longer allowed in certain areas, how do the teens feel about that? Do they think they have what they need to do their homework in the library? Are any spaces too quiet or too loud? Does the library need to have a vending machine? And so forth. That said, having a free time to discuss issues is a good idea, since you will not always be able to ask questions that address the most pressing issues to teens. But you should structure that time, too. Each person gets a certain amount of time to talk, or have an object that must be held in order to speak.

A TAB can also be less about issues and more about activities. In this case, the members of your TAB get together regularly to do something together. This could be a craft, a pizza party, or a contest of some kind—whatever they want to do. After the activity, the teens would have a chance to sit and eat and talk, about the library or anything they like. An activity-based TAB is more about bringing teens together in the library than anything else. This group may work best for you if you find that there are a lot of teens in the library with nothing to do. If they like being at the library but are bored or looking for something new, then find a common time and plan something every month—or more frequently, if you wish—for the teens to do together. In this case, you don't even have to call it a TAB. It could be a club of some kind. Let the kids come up with their own name.

Finally, a model I've found to be quite successful is a TAB that plans programs for other teens. Every month, the TAB gathers to talk about what events they would like to plan. The teens come up with the ideas that the librarian can veto, modify, or approve of. Some of their ideas won't be doable because of budgetary or staffing constraints, and some just need a few tweaks to get off the ground. In the past, the TAB I managed created a black-tie party, a cupcake social, and a talent competition, among other things. They also sometimes provided snacks at events and helped promote the library to their friends. The teens themselves had 90 percent of the control over these events. They planned them from start to finish, including assigning tasks to people. I was lucky in that they could purchase supplies and then be reimbursed, but this might not be possible in your community, which would mean that you would need to find another way to deal with purchases—either the teens give you a shopping list, or you accompany them to the store. An easier way around this is asking the teens to bake treats as opposed to buying them. The TAB executive board can be in charge of deciding who has to do what: set up and clean up, bringing snacks, publicity, calling performers, and so on. I recommend earmarking a certain amount of your budget for TAB events, meaning that the teens must divide this amount among all of their events. To this end, one member can be responsible for tracking his or her fellow members' spending.

ACTIVITIES

If you've got an activity-based TAB, you will find much information online and in print about what you might do with these teens. There are a few ways to approach this type of group:

- A library club is a group that gets together on a monthly basis to hang out, eat pizza, and talk—about books, the library, what's happening in town, and the like. This activity might rotate with special activities, some of which are listed below.
- Special activities could include anything—ask the teens what they want to do. Technology workshops, pizza taste tests, volunteering in the children's room, painting a mural—all of this might be fun for your teens. It's especially great if you can tie these activities back to the library's mission.
- You may find resources that suggest a theme-based schedule of events is the best way to plan TAB programs. While this idea holds merit (anti-Valentine's day poetry contests, making St. Patrick's day cards, a back-to-school party, etc.), remember to keep the focus more on the teens' interests than anything else.

OTHER WAYS TO INVOLVE TEENS

The Teen Advisory Board is not the only way to get teens formally involved in the library. Aside from fundraising and volunteer work, try forming other groups for teens to join.

The Teen Technology Committee

This group specifically advises you and other staff on the type of technology that should be implemented in the library. This group could also work on projects, either assigned by you or self-generated.

Advising. Teens, more than other user groups, stay up to date on current technology trends. You are probably aware that these trends seem to be focused on particular areas: mobile technology, gaming, gadgets, and so forth. Teens as a whole seem to be less interested in the nuts and bolts of technology, like software, than they do the flashy, fun stuff. However, if you're able to attract teens who are more into the behind-the-scenes tech stuff, take advantage of them! They may have more time than you do to keep up on the tech blogs, and they may catch things that fall between the cracks for you and others on your staff. Even if you don't have hard-core computer geeks in your group, you can ask the teens what they're hearing about new technology, and enlist them in brainstorming ways that technology can be used in the library.

I find that often it is the role of the librarian to suggest ideas, as teens will not always know that the library has the capability or the interest in using technology. But usually, once you get them started with a few out-of-the-box ideas, they can get rolling on their own. If the group really does have one of their ideas implemented, make sure they're recognized for it. Put it in your report to the board (or the director) and send a press release to the local paper.

Beta testing. If your library is trying out anything new in the tech realm, whether it's a new website, a new smart phone app, a database, or new circulating gadgets, get it into the hands of the teens first. Teens are great at trying things out fearlessly and teaching themselves how things work. They will be honest about what works and what doesn't work. Try to have them review new technology before it goes live—this will give you the opportunity to make changes before the service is available to the larger public.

Projects. A smart, motivated group of teens can work on specific projects for the library. You can manage this in a few ways. First, you could assign them specific tasks. For example, if you want a new page on your website where teens can post their writing and art, ask the group to design the page. Or, if you would like to start circulating digital cameras, have the group research which cameras would be best, based on certain criteria. Second, you could have the group work from a list of tasks, and pick and choose which they are most interested in. Ask your colleagues to help you create this list, based on the needs in their respective departments. Finally, if you have a very motivated bunch, ask them to generate their own list of ideas. This might come from interviewing staff members, spending time working in different departments, and/or testing features on the library website. The team could then run the list by you every so often to make sure that they are on the right track, and you might consider assigning one of them as the leader, to keep everyone organized and focused.

The Book-Buying Committee

The premise of this group is simple: get teens to recommend book purchases. This can definitely branch out to non-book purchases, and, in fact, getting advice on how to buy music, movies, and video games might be preferable. If possible, allow the teens a small budget and have them be responsible for staying within it. The group might meet monthly and be responsible for bringing lists of suggestions, and then discussing them before turning it over to you.

The Teen Advisory Board and groups like it can be one of the best ways for you, as a new librarian, to get to know the teens in your community and develop programs and services for them that will be as interesting and meaningful as possible. And over time, this group can develop to be a powerful body within the library.

6

◇ ◇ ◇

OUTREACH

You can have the best collection and programs in the world, but if no one knows about them, what's the point? Chances are, there are teens in your community who have been coming into the library their whole lives who are going to keep coming in; they might be thrilled about you being there, or they might be wary of change. Don't abandon them, but don't consider their presence enough. If there are teens in your community who don't use the library, you'll need to strategize about how to reach out to them and make them aware of what you're doing. In doing so, remember: bring the message to the teens, not the teens to the message. Teens who don't use the library probably don't visit the library's website, read about the library in the paper, or perk up their ears when people talk about the library. And, let's face it, teens who *do* use the library don't generally visit the website or read the paper, either. So what do you do?

INTRODUCING YOURSELF

Before we talk about how to get the word out, let's talk about what the word actually is. What are you trying to say? Why should teens care? What makes the library different, special, and appealing? Especially in communities where there are many options for teens, the library needs to make a name for itself. Opening a new teen area or starting a new teen program is exciting, so you can play off of that, but going beyond the initial flush of newness, how can you make sure the library stands out and is a choice that teens make often? In communities where there are lots of activities for teens, or organizations that cater to teens, then it could be hard for you to make a name for yourself. The library will be just one more place in town where teens can go, and people are not yet thinking of the library as a heavy hitter for teen services. But that all can change—it will take time, but it will happen.

Why the Library Is Special

First of all, *the library is free.* This isn't enough—in other words, mediocre services can't be justified by the fact that they are *free* mediocre services. But for teens, something free is something good. Teens do not always have access to a lot of disposable income. They may not be able to spend money on social activities or new books, games, or DVDs. For that reason, the library has a lot to offer them. While I don't think that "Free!" should be your number-one message, it's definitely something you should talk up. Not all teens—not all patrons, for that matter—know that library programs and materials are free.

The library offers teens choice. They have many options when they come to the library—they can choose from different activities, different reading materials, or different mediums. They can choose where they want to hang out in the library. This is not the case with other locations. Teens who hang out at home don't always have access to the same range of options, and where else can a teen find books, movies, games, and fun activities all in one place?

Truly, *the library is a youth-centered place.* This comes from you, the teen librarian. Teens will want to know that when they are in the library their opinions and needs matter. They will be able to make suggestions, and those suggestions will actually be considered. The staff will listen thoughtfully to teens and do everything they can to best serve them. Teens will have opportunities to serve on formal committees or just speak candidly with the staff. All of this is a crucial message—whenever you can, make sure that you are including this kind of information in your materials, if only in a quick line: "suggestions? E-mail Mary Smith at msmith@wood stocklibrary.org."

Finally, *the library is a safe space.* The staff works hard to make sure that bullying, name calling, abuse, and violence of any kind are never tolerated, and that all teens are welcome and appreciated. No teen should ever feel unsafe in the library for any reason. If you are committed to this, then this is something that teens should know about. It can be hard to articulate this, but work on trying to get a sense of safety across when you talk to teens or create any materials for distribution. It might be as easy as planning programs that appeal to a wide range of kids, or it could be done via booklists that appeal to different interests and backgrounds. Or, you could create a logo that says "The library is a safe space. Bullying is never tolerated." A library is staffed by people who care about teens and their well-being, and that should make any teen happy to be there.

Designing Your Outreach Materials

Teens pay attention to image. Nearly everything they see in the media is branded, from products to television to the Internet. Does your library have a brand? Can it be modified for the teen program? Ask someone in your library who knows—the publicity manager if there is one, or the director if there isn't. If your library doesn't have a brand, see if you can create one. Libraries that can afford to will hire an outside firm to create their brand, but if yours can't afford it, maybe someone on staff—you or someone else—can take that on. Here are some examples of libraries with terrific brands (thanks to myperfectlibrary.com for some of these, posted at http://myperfectlibrary.com/2009/10/31/cool-public-library-logos/):

- ImaginOn of the Public Library of Charlotte and Mecklenburg County http://www.imaginon.org.
- The Enoch Pratt Library http://www.prattlibrary.org/—see how they modified their logo for teens at http://teens.prattlibrary.org/.
- The Grand Rapids Public Library does such cool things with its website—each page is filled with a different pattern. The teen site is here: http://www.grpl.org/teens/. You'll want to click to each section.

If possible, once you've got a logo, use it on *everything* you put out for teens. The reason for this is simple: reinforcement. I hear so often that teens have no idea what's going on at the library, even though we've blanketed the town with flyers. They just may not associate the program with the library, even if they do notice the poster. Logos are a visual shortcut—they represent a lot in just one little image.

The design of specific materials says a lot about the library. Childish fonts and graphics will not appeal to teens. Depending on your audience, you may want your materials to look more mature—that is, something a savvy adult might be interested in—or more hip. And certainly, the design should change based on whatever it is you're promoting. It goes without saying that a skateboarding workshop should be advertised differently from an SAT workshop. Design can be intimidating, and there is a lot of bad design out there, so to help, here are some free resources you can consult for advice and inspiration:

- Presentation Zen (http://www.presentationzen.com/) is the blog of Garr Reynolds, whose book by the same title is a bible for many who design slides and other materials for presentations, and he also touches on marketing and other print materials. His blog contains a list of recommended books that is worth perusing. The "Design Basics" section of his personal website (http://www.garr reynolds.com/Design) is an excellent essay on good design and he links to other sites with design tips.

- The Library Signage photo pool on Flickr (http://www.flickr.com/ groups/librarysignage/) is a great place to see well-done—and not-so-well-done—signs. Along the same lines, read the posts on Michael Stephen's blog, Tame the Web, that are tagged "signage in libraries," at http://tametheweb.com/category/signage-in-lib raries/. You will find many examples of poor signs and design here, but also some examples of good ones.

- How to Design a Print Ad (http://www.newsletterfillers.com/ archives/advertising/how_to_design_print_ad.htm). While this article is about creating print ads for newsletters, the basic principles apply to any kind of print advertising.

- The Building Blocks of Great Composition (http://www.allgra phicdesign.com/graphicsblog/2010/06/the-building-blocks-of-great-composition/) is a concise article on easy ways to make your print materials look more professional and polished.

- The Youth Marketing Channel on YPulse (http://www.ypulse. com/category/youth-marketing) contains an amazing list in the right-hand sidebar listing dozens of youth marketing companies. Click through these to get ideas about what's trendy, popular, and effective in marketing materials to teens.

To find interesting and non-clichéd art for your materials, go to Flickr. If you use Flickr's Creative Commons search by visiting http://www.flickr. com/search/advanced/ and clicking the box next to "Only search within

Creative Commons-licensed content," you will get thousands of images that you are free to use in your publicity! Searching for "free clip art" on Google will get you loads of results, some useable, some not. Also consider using a teen artist to create logos and illustrations for materials.

And finally, if you have the money, use a design firm. Your library may already enlist the help of professionals for other materials, like fundraising postcards or event series pamphlets, so ask if you can have at least one thing added to the list. Choose wisely—make it something big, like summer reading or your fall programming lineup, a flyer to attend the grand opening of the new teen space, or a pamphlet that outlines all the cool stuff that can be seen and done in the teen space.

SOCIAL NETWORKING

Your library absolutely *must* have an online presence that is not your website. Yes, your website is lovely, and yes, it's a great place to promote programs, but really, if teens aren't visiting it, it's not enough. And here's a tip: they're not visiting it. There may be a small core group that goes to the site, and there may be teens who go to the site to get information about library hours or get a phone number, but they are likely not using the website to find program listings, watch videos, or read book reviews. I'm sure there are a few exceptions to this rule if people at your library have been working especially hard to drive traffic to the site, but they are just that—exceptions. If no one has been targeting teens thus far, then trust me: teens aren't visiting your site.

This doesn't mean you should stop posting content to your library's website. It just means that you need to be linking that content to outside social networks. Both Twitter and Facebook allow for posts to be linked to each other and external sites, depending on what you use for your content management system. Ask your Web designer if this is possible. The point is to both draw teens to the library's website and reach teens who aren't doing that already. This can be a complex process, so if you can, draw up a plan for developing your online presence. Once you read through the sections below, you should have an idea of how you want to tackle that.

The Parameters of Your Online Presence

A debate rages—or at least murmurs—among librarians about how to manage the library's online presence. It's personal accounts versus professional accounts; Figures 6.1 and 6.2 summarize the two arguments in a nutshell.

PROS	CONS
Teens will see the "real" you, which will make you easier for them to connect with and relate to.	Teens might see personal information about you that you are uncomfortable sharing with them.
You will only have to update one profile and will avoid the annoyance of maintaining multiple accounts.	Parents could feel uncomfortable with you, as an adult, being friends online with a minor.
You will have credibility and not look like you're either a stalker or someone who only works at the library.	Teens might not be comfortable with being friends with an adult online.
	You will have to spend time adjusting your privacy settings so that teens are not privy to information you consider too personal for them to see.

Figure 6.1: Using personal accounts.

PROS	CONS
You never have to worry about privacy issues.	If you're not careful, your profile will be dull and make it look as though all you do is work and talk about the library.
You can talk about library stuff all the time without driving your real friends crazy.	When you try to friend teens, they may be wary to accept since you will have few other friends online.

Figure 6.2: Using professional accounts.

Facebook

Facebook is currently the number one social media site around, and you absolutely should consider it as part of your online strategy. Facebook is the second-most visited website worldwide, behind only Google,[1] and about 35 percent of its users are between the ages of 13 and 24—about 36 million users.[2] For that reason alone, your library should have a presence on Facebook, and you should, too. Many of your teen patrons will be using Facebook, and anything you post on the site could be seen by them. I think that often it is best to post things as an individual (though you should carefully consider the pros and cons in the arguments about personal accounts versus professional accounts), because teens may pay more attention to that than if information comes from the library as an institution. It is very easy to set up a page for your library, though you will need to have an account in order to do so. You will want to include as much information about the library as possible—hours, location, and the like—and include a profile photo. Photos of the library, or of the teen area, are good.

So what do you do with a Facebook page? Well, for one thing, you need to use it actively in order to have any impact at all. Assign the page a moderator—likely, this will be you. Go onto the site every day. This helps with maintaining your account, as you may have friend requests, messages, or event invitations to respond to. You will also want to watch the traffic on your page and pay attention to who is becoming a fan of your library's page and if any comments are being posted on it. When you post, make sure that you are not just posting "ads" for events. Post links to funny videos or news articles, make little comments about what's happening in the library or some new books that just came in—give the library some personality. You will begin to see teens become fans of the library. You will also see adults and other librarians liking your page, and that's OK, though really your main audience should be teens.

A fun way to draw teens to your Facebook page is to hold contests. Teens who become friends of or comment on the library's page can be entered in a drawing, for example. Or, hold a virtual book discussion right on your wall. You might also have teens post the answers to a quiz or scavenger hunt there. Anything to drive traffic. To find out detailed information about traffic on your page, go to your Insights Dashboard (https://www.facebook.com/insights/). This page allows you to see statistics about activity surrounding your page—fans, comments, likes, and so on. These can be great stats to show your administrators.

TAB Group Online

Create a group for your teen advisory board. To create a group, click on the "groups" link on the left-hand side of the main Facebook page and then click the "Create a Group" button. Fill out all the fields and you're done. If you are friends with your TAB members on Facebook, invite them to join—if not, you can send them an e-mail invite. You can also tell them about it in person at your next meeting. Not all teens have Facebook accounts, though, so you don't want to use this group for all essential information and not duplicate that anywhere. Teens could feel left out this way. Once you have a group in place, this group can send out event invites, which lends those invites an air of credibility.

Twitter

Twitter is still not being used by teens anywhere near as much as Facebook, though the numbers are growing—according to Quantcast.com, 14 percent of users are between the ages of 13 and 17.[3] Twitter is more a tool for you—it is a great way to connect with other librarians and area professionals, and many people use Twitter in the same way that you might use a feed reader, since a lot of sites now have Twitter accounts that stream their updates and posts. That said, don't hesitate to use Twitter to advertise and connect. The best part about Twitter is that you can easily link it up to your Facebook page. So, any time you post to Facebook, the post gets blasted out to Twitter with a link to the post itself. Go to http://www.facebook.com/twitter/ to do this. It's pretty cool, and it saves you a ton of time. If you want to go in the other direction—having your Twitter updates post to your Facebook page—add the Selective Tweets app: https://www.facebook.com/selectivetwitter.

Others: YouTube, Vimeo, and More

Facebook and Twitter get talked about the most, but here are some other sites for you to keep in mind.

- Everyone knows YouTube. It's a fantastic place to find funny videos, but it's also a fantastic place to post the library's videos. Create a YouTube channel for your library by creating an account that uses your library's name and the word *teen*—so, awesome libraryteen. Then upload all of your teen videos. Share the link—in my example, http://www.youtube.com/user/woodstocklibrary teen—on your website and Facebook page. Teens can watch and also comment and favorite your videos.
- Vimeo is another video sharing site, and it looks a little slicker than YouTube. I also think it's easier to embed Vimeo videos on websites than it is YouTube videos. Go to www.vimeo.com. You can create groups and channels—so, a channel just for teens, or just for the TAB, or just for certain types of events, and so on. You can view statistics on how many people have watched your

videos, either on the Vimeo site or the embedded videos on your own site.

- Foursquare is the best known of the location-based social networks. Others include Gowalla, Loopt, and BrightKite; Facebook has also added a "check in" functionality to its website. In Foursquare, users download an application to their smart phone and then use it to check in at various locations they visit. This is a way to connect with others who are in the same area and show their friends what they're up to. Many libraries are getting in on the Foursquare phenomenon, offering prizes for people who check in to the library the most. Visit http://foursquare.com/.

OTHER FORMS OF VIRTUAL OUTREACH

Social media is not the only way to reach out to teens who are not physically in the library, though you may need to use social media to help you promote these services.

Texting

Teens use cell phones more than any other piece of technology available. Even in areas where the digital divide is a powerful thing, teens have cell phones. Even non-smartphones have texting capability, and teens text more than they call. If you want to reach the largest number of teens possible, use text messaging to do it. Texting might seem intimidating, but it's really not difficult. There are easy, cheap ways of texting and more complex, more expensive ways of texting. Start with the former and if it's working, consider moving on to the latter.

You'll start out with just being able to send texts one way: out. To send text messages to teens, you first need their cell phone numbers. Speak with your administrators about this, and come up with a way to start gathering cell phone numbers. You can do this by asking teens at programs to sign in and provide their number if they want, having some kind of form on your website, and sending out e-blasts about it.

Note: Teens need to know that text messaging fees could apply and that you will never use their cell phone number for anything except sending them information about the library. You may also wish to have them fill out a form that their parent signs, in case you are worried about parents not wanting their children's phone numbers handed out.

Once you have their cell phone numbers, you can send messages to teens' phones very easily. All you have to do is compose a message that is under 140 characters and send it to the teens' cell phone numbers. A crucial piece of information here is their provider. You will need to get this information when you get their number. Here are the e-mail formats for different mobile providers:

- AT&T: number@txt.att.net
- Qwest: number@qwestmp.com
- T-Mobile: number@tmomail.net
- Verizon: number@vtext.com
- Sprint: number@messaging.sprintpcs.com or number@pm.sprint.com
- Virgin Mobile: number@vmobl.com
- Nextel: number@messaging.nextel.com
- Alltel: number@message.alltel.com
- Metro PCS: number@mymetropcs.com
- Powertel: number@ptel.com
- Suncom: number@tms.suncom.com
- U.S. Cellular: number@email.uscc.net

Keep adding these numbers to a distribution list, and then it becomes easy to just blast out messages to the whole list every time you want to promote something. Be careful, though, about over-messaging, and make sure teens know that all they have to do is ask you and you'll remove their number from the list.

Once you're ready to move on to text messaging services that allow teens to text you back, you have some options:

- Consider getting the library a cell phone and hand out its number to teens. Get an unlimited texting plan. You'll only use the phone when you're in the library, so let teens know it's not a 24-hour service.
- If you use LibraryH3lp—a multi-user chat service—for IMing with patrons, you can link LibraryH3lp and Google Voice to have text messages come through your IM portal. Read this for more information: http://libraryh3lp.blogspot.com/2009/08/google-voice-sms-gateway.html. It's free!
- If you're ready, call Mosio, the company that created Text a Librarian: http://www.textalibrarian.com/. There are a lot of options

available to you here, from outgoing texts only to two-way texting services. There is a set-up fee and a monthly fee.

Instant Messaging (IM)

Making IM services available to teens (and patrons of all ages, for that matter) is extremely simple. IM is not really the right medium for mass outreach, but it does make the library more available and accessible, and just the act of offering IM services makes a statement about the library's interest in catering to the needs of teens. The best way to offer IM is through a service that aggregates all of the different IM channels—like AIM, Yahoo, Google Chat, and so on. Here are a couple worth looking into. They both offer widgets, or tools that can be embedded onto your library's website to allow users to IM you right from the page.

- LibraryH3lp. They ask for a one-time donation of $100. Easy to use, though it takes someone with some tech skills to get it set up. The nice thing about LH is that is allows for different queues, which means that users can IM different departments, and departments can forward IMs to each other. You can also monitor IM transcripts easily through the admin page. http://libraryh3lp. blogspot.com/
- Meebo. Meebo is cool because it offers support for smartphones, so your users can IM you on the go. Meebo also has chat rooms, where multiple people can gather and chat. This could be a wonderful way to run a virtual book discussion.

Make sure you advertise both IM and text services all over the place. Include this information on your print materials and in a tagline at the end of press releases. Print out MOO mini business cards with your information on them and hand them out to teens. Post this information on the library's website, and tell all the teens you meet in the library. Word of mouth will spread about this service, and before you know it, teens will be IMing you like crazy and signing up to get your texts.

GOING INTO THE SCHOOLS

So where are the teens? Well, by now you should know a little bit about your community and what teens like to do in their free time. And you certainly know where they are for about eight hours a day, Monday through Friday. Let's start there: the schools. If you're a school librarian, this advice still applies; in fact, you're already on campus with the teachers, so you're ahead of the game.

Many schools list contact information for their teachers on their websites. Not all teachers respond to cold call e-mails, but some of them do, and all you need is one connection to start. Teachers are so busy that they might be more likely to respond to a specific invitation to collaborate than a general sentiment that you'd love to work together. That said, it could work if you e-mail a few select departments to introduce yourself and invite the teachers to visit your new teen space. You never know—they might have an idea just waiting for a collaborator. I've had most luck with projects that are academic-related, like a teen writing competition. Ask if you can attend a department meeting or visit classrooms to promote the program.

Hold an open house for teachers at the library with coffee and pastries. It might work best to get word out through the administration. A new teen program is a good excuse to start talking about working together. Target specific teachers in the schools. It's intuitive: doing an art project? Let the art department know. Is there a film club? Call the group's advisor when it's time to hold a movie contest or screen anime. Invite their ideas, too—it can't be a one-way conversation or it won't work. A simple "I'm thinking about doing some kind of music program at the library—would you be interested in brainstorming with me?" is a great way to start. If you're in a new building, it's a good excuse to hold a tour. I planned one and a million great ideas came out of it, including showing films in our new auditorium as part of the sophomore English curriculum, giving space free of charge to a math teacher who wanted to offer extra help during exams, and connecting with a Mandarin teacher about getting a Chinese-language group up and running.

Don't forget your friend the school librarian. Many school librarians don't have time in the day to focus on cultural programming or extracurricular support, so they might welcome the chance to send their students your way after school. Ask if you can place flyers in the school library, and be sure to reciprocate when they need a partner in the community. The school librarians can also be a good starting point for you when you're not sure whom to reach out to. If you're wondering who could help you drum up a panel of high school athletes to talk about the college admissions process, the school librarian can tell you which coach to get in touch with.

All this is well and good for connecting and collaborating with adults, but how about teens? Isn't that the whole point? Well, if you can get yourself into the classroom, you're reaching a nice number. Not all of them will care about what you have to say, but some of them really will. Bring in flyers—yes, you'll see many in the recycling bin at the end of the day, but again, not all of them. Ask for five minutes at the beginning of class to pitch a program and leave your materials for anyone who's interested. Don't talk for too long—just give yourself enough time to get the point across and seem nice.

Booktalking

Booktalks are an excellent way to reach huge numbers of teens. I've given booktalks to small groups of single classes and huge groups of six classes at once. There may already be a tradition of the children's librarians giving booktalks in the elementary schools—or even the middle schools—so it should be a simple transition to expand this service to teens. While I admit that I have never booktalked to high school students, only middle school students, I know many librarians who have—and love it. Some schools will have librarians go from classroom to classroom, while others will gather multiple classes in the school library. I would recommend starting with the school librarian for this process; be aware that the school library may already be providing this service and not wish to collaborate, but definitely ask. If booktalks take place at the beginning of major programming initiatives, like at the end of the school year, take advantage of the audience and bring your summer reading brochures or anything else you might wish to promote.

I have had great luck with allowing students to take out books straight from the booktalk. This only works if you are visiting a single group; otherwise, it's not fair to the earlier groups to send books home only with the last group. If you can bring your laptop and open up your ILS on it, great—if not, just write down names and item barcodes. If you really don't feel comfortable circulating remotely, at least take down names and place holds on items when you get back to the library. I have found that when you hold up a book and say, "Who wants this?" there is a mad rush to grab it, which is fun to see and also a great peer endorsement of reading and the library.

An extension of remote circulation during book talking is remote services, period. Set up camp in the lunchroom (which is scary—bring a colleague if it makes you feel less awkward) with a laptop, a stack of books, and a stack of flyers. And maybe a bowl of treats. If your library has an IM service, have it open so that you can get help with reference questions you can't answer on your own. Provide reader's advisory service, check out books, talk up your programs, and just say hi. Be prepared to take down e-mail addresses or cell phone numbers; and if you have a Facebook page, Twitter account, or any other social networking presence, have those Web pages open and show them off. This can happen anywhere—not just the schools. Is there a teen center in town? Or a coffee shop that's really hopping after school? See if they would allow you to visit once a month—once a week—whatever everyone's schedule can accommodate.

There are some excellent resources available for novice booktalkers. Books include:

Bromann, Jennifer. *More Booktalking that Works.* New York: Neal Schuman, 2005.
Cox-Clark, Ruth. *Tantalizing Tidbits for Teens: Quick Booktalks for the Busy High School Library Media Specialist,* volumes 1 and 2. Santa Barbara: Linworth, 2002 and 2007.
Langemack, Chapple. *The Booktalker's Bible: How to Talk About the Books You Love to Any Audience.* Santa Barbara: Libraries Unlimited, 2003.
Mahood, Kristine. *Booktalking with Teens.* Westport, CT: Libraries Unlimited, 2010.

For booktalks found online, try the following websites:

Shenandoah Public Library's Teen Book Talks: http://www.shenan doah.lib.ia.us/teenbooktalks.html

Nancy Keane's Booktalks—Quick and Simple: http://nancykeane. com/booktalks/ya.htm

The YA YA YAs' Booktalking Tips (with links to online booktalks): http://theyayayas.wordpress.com/2008/10/15/booktalking-tips-2008/

School Clubs

Take a peek at the local middle and high school's web pages. Do they have any groups that could work with you on a particular project? You can look at this two ways: one, you can plan a program and then see if there are groups you can promote it to; and two, you can see what groups are out there and then base a program around that particular interest. Some examples of both:

- Visit the literary magazine, school newspaper, or poetry clubs to promote writing competitions.
- If you are making any video content, ask the video or AV club if they want to get involved.
- If there are any cultural or social groups in the schools—a gay/lesbian alliance, for example, or a film club—then think about what kinds of programs and services they might be interested

in. Discussion groups, book lists, programs? Could any of these groups use library space for their activities, like meetings or film screenings or performances?

- Along those lines, see if the drama or music groups would ever like to rehearse in the library or put on one show there in a series. Musical groups can be especially sweet in library lobbies or courtyards—a music lunch break, for example.
- If the school hosts community service or internship groups, see if you can get on a list of organizations looking for help.

Library Orientations

This can be tricky, as chances are the school library is already doing orientations for new students, or covering those topics in library units. However, just because they're doing it doesn't mean you can't. After all, the public and school libraries have different resources, layout, and staff. There's no reason why students shouldn't be familiar with their public library, too. If you are interested in doing this, I would recommend reaching out to the teachers in either the English or history departments, because they tend to assign the most research projects. It's best to call or drop in if you already have spoken with them; e-mail tends to get lost in the shuffle.

If teachers are interested, they may wish to bring their students by on a field trip, or assign them the task of visiting the library on their own, outside of school hours. Here are two sample agendas for both scenarios:

Class visits. In a sense, this is easier, because you will see all of the students at once and have the opportunity to interact with them all more. If you have 40 minutes, here's my suggestion for how to break down the time:

1. Introduce yourself and the library. Discuss the library's hours, the names of the staff, where you can find the OPACs, and what you need to access the databases. Also tell the students how to get a library card (10 minutes)

2. Give a quick tour of the reference area and the teen area (10 minutes)

3. Give each student an assignment to find one fact about a topic using a particular resource and give them a 10-minute time limit.

4. When the students rejoin each other, ask for volunteers to explain how they found their fact. Have everyone turn in their assignment to their teacher (10 minutes)

Assignment: Have each student draw a topic out of one hat and a resource out of another hat. Topics could include historical events, famous people, inventions and scientific discoveries, locations, and so on. Don't get too esoteric; they only have 10 minutes. Resources could include an encyclopedia, a website, a database, a book, a magazine. Make sure you have pointed out where all of these things can be found during your tour and/or introduction.

Individual visits: Modify the above so that each time a student visits the library, they have to check off that they have seen certain important areas of the library. This will allow them to explore on their own; you won't have to drop everything each time a student drops in. In essence, what you are creating is a scavenger hunt that requires the student to write down a unique piece of information about different areas of and resources in the library. This proves that they have actually explored those areas. You might ask them to write down the call number of a book in a certain area, name three magazines and newspapers the library subscribes to, find a fact using an encyclopedia, write down the name of a book found in the OPAC, tell you the name of two databases, and so forth. Once this is done, you can go over the answers with the student and see if they have any questions for you. You can then grade or approve the worksheet and the student will hand it to their teacher in class the next day.

In both cases, it can be worthwhile to not only focus on areas of the library that support academics, but also to let teens know about the YA book collection, the kinds of programs you offer, how to get involved in the teen advisory board, and the like. In many cases, this will be your only chance to interact with some of these students, and you should take advantage of it. Have the tour end in the teen area, for example, and hand out MOO cards with your contact information or flyers with upcoming events on it. Make sure that the teens visit the library's website and the teen page on the website, and make sure they know which social networks the library is using.

Promoting Events

Getting into the schools is one of the best ways to promote certain events. You can't do it for everything, and your best chance of getting teachers to allow you into their classrooms is if the event you are promoting is vaguely school-related. For example, visit English classes to talk up the library's teen writing competition, and encourage teens to enter pieces that they had written for school in the contest. Teachers, chances are, are happy to do this if it involves an activity that enriches or supplements their students' school experiences. Sometimes teachers will even offer extra credit to their students who do participate. Other examples might be poetry workshops, computer design classes, tutoring sessions, college prep seminars, panels on Internet safety, robotics programs, and art, music, or drama programs. Be specific about which teachers you contact—the math teachers, chances are, don't want to hear about a yoga class you're doing, but the gym teachers might be interested.

OTHER COMMUNITY PARTNERSHIPS
Youth Groups

Depending on your community, you may find that tons of youth groups already exist. Examples are Students against Destructive Decisions (SADD), church and synagogue youth groups, and non-school-based community service groups (some community service organizations have junior groups for kids and teens), and youth boards. You may also find club sports and youth sports associations, youth theater groups, non-school academic groups, and so on. It can be hard to figure out what all of these things are, so spend some time doing research online about your community, and also ask around. The schools may have information about these outside groups, as might town hall or other town offices. If your community has an office for youth services, stop by their office to chat about how you might work with them or get ideas about different agencies.

Partnering with these groups can be an excellent way to reach out and make inroads into your community. Many youth organizations will be well-established, with large memberships and involved teens and parents. Even running one joint program would go a long way toward increasing your visibility in the community and showing that you are interested in collaboration and supporting the mission of those who care about teens in your community. Programs might include discussion groups, joint community service projects, or clinics—for example, the youth lacrosse league might hold a workshop on stringing lacrosse stick heads at the library. Or the theater group could run a mini-class on improv, makeup for the stage, or audition tips. Groups like Odyssey of the Mind and SADD can use library space, and perhaps if you run an event to raise money for the library, you could co-sponsor with SADD and raise money for them, too. Teens who are highly involved in these groups tend to like being involved, so they are the perfect people for you to reach out to at first—they will most likely want to get involved with the library as well. And the more you reach out, the more you will come across teens who might *not* come into the library already. A teen who is wholly committed to their church group might not take the time to visit the library, but once they see that the library has things they are looking for, too, that could change. It is a way to both build a base and expand your reach.

Parent Associations

Again, this will vary by community, but in some cities and towns, parents are highly involved in their children's schooling and extracurricular activities. In that case, you will find parent organizations at different schools, as well as groups dealing specifically with youth issues. Sometimes the PTA (Parent Teacher Association) is different from a parents' network, which is often a larger group of parents who are looking for information about the schools—this as opposed to the PTA, which is usually an official body that has some effect on policy. In all cases, you can get yourself to those meetings. When you first start your job, contact someone at these organizations to see if you can get on the agenda for just five minutes—enough time to introduce yourself, let everyone know how happy you are to be in the library, and explain some of your interests and philosophies very briefly. If you explain that you are willing and excited to work with other organizations in town, you may be surprised by the number of people who approach you after the meeting to chat with you about ideas they have.

Once you lay some groundwork, you will find that the parents' groups are great places to go for specific ideas. If there's a project you want to work on and you need help, or buy-in, the parents might be the place to go. Programs for parents and teens, like book groups or investment clubs, or programs just for parents, or of interest to parents, like college admissions information or teen finance classes, can be promoted through parent groups and you may also find some volunteers or ideas in the bunch. If you can ever co-sponsor a program with a parent organization, do it. You will do wonders for your position in the community and hugely increase your visibility. If you are in a community where parents get involved, then you want parents on your side and interested in the library.

You might also consider visiting them on a regular basis—once or twice a year—to update them on what's happening at the library for teens. You can talk about summer reading, big programs, new initiatives, and so on. While you're there, have parents give you their contact information if they're interested in hearing more, and stick around for the whole meeting to make sure you can network at the end.

I should mention that all of these meetings are also fantastic ways to find out about what's happening in your community—so it's worth attending as a spectator even if you're not presenting anything.

Businesses

Flyers in the library are great, but as I said before, if the kids aren't coming in anyway, then putting flyers on the circ desk won't do a thing. Instead, advertise at local coffee shops, pizza places, popular stores, movie theaters, and gyms or rec centers. And while you're there, see if you can chat with the store manager. Many stores and businesses, especially big ones, have people on staff who only work on community outreach. Aside from donating prizes and snacks, businesses might have some great ideas for working with the library. Some examples:

- See if your local grocery store would like to co-sponsor a teen cooking program, or a program on vegetarian food, or local food. Perhaps someone on their staff could come in to teach the teens.

- Bookstores are a no-brainer. Co-sponsor author visits, book discussions, or writing workshops. If you do have an author visit, ask the bookstore to sell copies of the author's books for signing after the talk.

- Clothing stores might be interested in joining forces on cultural programs. Funky, alternative shops might want to get in on a skateboarding workshop, for example. More mainstream shops could co-sponsor a jewelry-making class or a workshop on fashion design. Maybe someone on their staff could lead it.

- Coffee shops could definitely sponsor a late-night study session or open mic night.

- Music stores, game stores, or electronics stores might like to sponsor a gaming tournament, songwriting contest, or video contest. Employees could be judges, or offer tips and advice.

- Businesses of all sorts could send a representative to a career fair or panel discussion. Marketing, sales, law, finance, design—if you have these businesses in your community, ask them if they want to get involved.

- Along the same lines, see if you can organize some kind of internship or apprenticeship program with local businesses. It could be short—a week, a couple of days—and in the summer. Teens could spend time trying out different jobs. And the library could have an internship available, too.

PRESS

Writing press releases can be time consuming and stressful—keeping it all straight is hard. Depending on where you are, there could be multiple places where you'll want publicity, from print newspapers to local bloggers to community calendars. I recommend two things: one, keep all of your press releases on file and use them as templates. There's no reason to reinvent the wheel (and if someone is already writing press releases for your library, you should definitely speak to them and perhaps use their write-ups as a template). Two, keep organized. Keep a spreadsheet with all of your events and a checklist of areas where you can send press releases. Be aware of deadlines—put those on the spreadsheet, too. Then, at some regular interval, once a week or twice a month, check your spreadsheet and run down the list.

Who's Reading Your Press?

It depends on where you're publishing stuff, but really, if we're talking about traditional news sources—and included in that are blogs, because teens don't typically read blogs—then the people who are reading your press releases are adults. But before you decide to not even bother, remember that adults often have children—teenaged children. Think carefully about your community, though. Do you live in an area where parents are heavily involved in their teens' activities? Do parents encourage their kids to go to the library? The older teens get, the less influence their parents have on them, so if you're hosting an event for middle school students, newspaper articles might be a good thing; for juniors and seniors in high school, maybe alternate channels are better.

I mention this because when you write press releases for traditional news outlets, keep your audience in mind. You don't have to be edgy, funny, or cool if your information is going to be read by parents. Just include all of the pertinent details and a nice description so that parents know exactly what the event is all about. Make sure to include age restrictions if there are any. And always include contact information so that parents can call you if they have questions.

I can't think of many examples of media outlets that are read by teens—I think most of your publicity that is intended to go straight to teens should be on Facebook, Twitter, your library's website, and via e-mail, text, and direct contact (either through school visits or some other connection, or in the library). But you should still use the newspapers if they are read in your community. Parents will tell their children about what they read, and articles or listings in the paper are also a form of promotion. Even if people aren't spreading the word about the library to teens, they are still learning that the library is a go-to place for services to teens, and that is an important message for you to get into your community.

Sample Press Release

Here is a sample press release that may be useful to you—but again, make sure you see what others have already done for your library. All libraries have specific requirements for their PR, such as including the library's slogan, or the address and phone number, or something else. This is just an example of one way of writing a press release.

For release: June 15, 2010
  From: Jen Smith, Awesome Library, 555-6543 [director] Sam Jones, Woodstock Library, 555-3459 [teen librarian]

Teens can chat with bestselling author, plus share writing at Woodstock Library

On Monday, June 22 from 6 p.m. to 7 p.m., teens in grades 6 through 8 are invited to attend Woodstock Library's first Middle School Book Discussion of the summer. The book being discussed is *Life as We Knew It* by Susan Beth Pfeffer. Ms. Pfeffer will be calling the library during the discussion so that teens can ask her questions about writing and her books. Pizza will be served. Please register for this event, which will be held in the teen room.

On Wednesday, June 4 from 7 to 8:30 p.m., Woodstock Library will host an open mic night for teens ages 13 and up. Teens are invited to bring original musical works to share, either instrumental or vocal, and must provide their own instruments. Teens who would prefer to listen are welcome as well. Coffee, tea, and pastries will be served. Registration for this event, which will be held in the auditorium, is not required.

Woodstock Library is located at 1234 Main St. For more information, call 555-1234 or visit woodstocklibrary.net.

Sample Blog Post

For your own website or for websites or blogs that are read by people in your area, you can be more casual. Websites will want to publish short blurbs, not long articles, so it's important to boil your message down to the basics. You might also include a photo or graphic since those are more likely to be published online than in print. For example, here's a rewriting of the above press release for a blog or website:

Woodstock Library is hosting two great events for teens next week. On Monday, June 22 at 6 p.m., author Susan Beth Pfeffer will be calling our Middle School Book Discussion. Ms. Pfeffer will answer questions about writing and her books. The book being discussed if Ms. Pfeffer's *Life as We Knew It*. Pizza will be served. Please register for this event, which will be held in the teen room.

On Wednesday, June 4 at 7 p.m., we're hosting an open mic night for teens ages 13 and up. Bring original musical works to share, either instrumental or vocal, and please bring your own instruments. Teens can also come to listen and enjoy coffee, tea, and pastries. You do not need to register for this event. Questions? Call Sarah at 555-3659 or e-mail sludwig@woodstocklibrary.net.

Sample PR Schedule

As I mentioned above, it's really important to stay organized when it comes to publicity. Figure 6.3 provides a sample checklist you might be able to modify and use.

Don't forget that, as I mentioned in the section on social networking, you can often connect your social networks so that content posted in one place is also posted to other sites without you having to do it yourself.

		Newspaper	E-blast	Website	Flyers	Facebook	Twitter
Open Mic Night 6/15	Deadline	6/2	6/12	6/8	6/1	6/8	6/10 and 6/15
	Done?	x		x	x	x	
Book Discussion 6/23	Deadline	6/9	6/19	6/15	6/8	6/13	6/17 and 6/23
	Done?	x			x		

Figure 6.3: Sample PR schedule.

This makes it easy to stay on top of your different advertising venues. At the same time, perhaps if you send a press release to the newspaper, it will also get to the person in charge of the paper's events calendar.

CHALLENGES WITH OUTREACH

Among other challenges, outreach sometimes becomes the one part of your jobs that gets pushed most to the side. When you are faced with the immediate tasks of programming, collection development, and budgeting, it's not always easy to focus on thinking of new ways to create partnerships and develop new audiences. Try to remember that outreach is one of the most important things you do. Without it, all of the work you spend on the rest of your job will not be as effective as it could be. Carve time out of your day, every day, to hammer away at outreach. Keep a list of different community groups that you might reach out to and check them off as you speak with them. Tack a copy of your PR schedule up to your bulletin board. And put it on your to-do list.

Reaching Out to Teachers and Librarians

Having been on both sides of this issue, both as a public and school librarian, I am sympathetic to the school librarians and teachers who struggle to find time in their tight schedules to work with public librarians. And now that I am a public librarian, I find myself sometimes frustrated by how difficult it can be to partner with teachers. I think there are a few issues here. One, teachers are often locked into rigid schedules and have very little time during the day to follow up on e-mails and phone calls. Two, teachers—and school librarians—have their own plans and agenda for their programs, and sometimes it's hard for them to collaborate if it means giving up some control. I certainly don't mean this in a negative way, since of course I have been in that position—I speak from experience. When a school librarian is trying to develop an innovative program, an offer to collaborate from a librarian in a separate institution might not be a welcome intrusion. If you find yourself getting the vibe that the person you're trying to connect with isn't as interested as you might like, at some point it's worth backing off. Being too persistent will not make you any allies. Move on to someone else in the school.

If you have a solid connection at the school library, start there. The school librarian knows everyone and sees a ton of students come through his door every day. If you can set up regular meetings with him, this could be a great way to check in and brainstorm. Ask him to introduce you to colleagues who are open to working on projects together, as well as to kids who love the library. See if he can get you to a faculty meeting to speak with all of the teachers about the public library and what you can offer them. Slowly, you will start to get to know the teachers and build relationships with them, so that you can have go-to people when it comes to wanting to try out a new idea.

The other challenge involved in working with teachers, of course, is the fact that they are not available during one of the busiest times at the library—the summer. While this can be frustrating when you are trying to promote a new program or initiative, keep the faith that the summer is also when kids are the most likely to come into the library. They are used to attending summer reading programs as children, and kids who aren't at camp or in summer school need things to do. You can definitely find other ways to reach out to them during these times. While you probably won't be able to collaborate with teachers over the summer, you might try asking some of them if they would be willing to teach a class for summer reading (for a fee, of course, to sweeten the deal). And if there is anything you would like to work on with teachers in the fall, you'll want to start sowing the seeds in the spring, before school vacation starts. Over the summer, check in via e-mail.

Reaching Out to a Broad Demographic

There are already teens coming into the library—I guarantee it. They may be a certain group of friends, or teens with similar interests. For whatever reason, they enjoy coming into the library, or have nowhere else to go. It's a great idea to start with these kids. Approach them, introduce yourself, tell them you're open to their ideas, and ask them if there is anything you can do for them (but don't be too heavy-handed). If these teens are receptive, you may find yourself with a loyal following. It would be very easy to just focus on these teens, or on the first group of teens that you are able to entice into the library. If you are like most teen librarians, you will eventually find yourself in a situation where you have the same group of teens coming in all the time and taking place in the same kind of activities all the time. All teen areas have their regulars. This is totally normal. But it is very important to make sure that you are offering a broad range of programs for a broad range of teens. It's easy to fall back on the needs and desires of your regulars, but that means that there are a ton of teens with different interests whom you aren't reaching.

When it comes to outreach, there are a few things you can do to try to stay well-rounded: talk to people from many different organizations. Visit different clubs at the schools. Offer programs for teens who will be going on to college and teens who will not. And make sure that you are reaching the teens who are *not* involved in clubs and other organizations. Do not rely on that kind of outreach for everything that you do, but instead make sure you are finding ways to reach out to the teens who go home after school, or work, or just hang out with friends. And sometimes, too, the teens who are heavily involved in academics and sports are hard to reach, because they spend so much of their time studying or at practice. In other words, don't spend all of your energy on the teens who one might expect to be in the library—the artsy kids, the readers, the alternative kids, the—for lack of better word—geeks and nerds (terms I use with the greatest of affection, since I count myself as one of them). All teens are welcome in the library and for that reason, you will have to make sure your outreach efforts are reaching teens of all sorts, and that the message you are sending is that no group or clique is valued above any others. If you find that the library is being used by the same teens over and over, take some time to step back, evaluate what it is you're doing that is attractive to these teens, and strategize what you can do to reach out to others.

Advocating for Social Media

If you are coming up against some resistance toward developing a social media presence, be prepared to whip out the stats and evidence. Administrators may be uncomfortable with using sites like Facebook and Twitter in an official capacity. This is understandable; there's a lot of negative backlash out there about social networking, and why would the library want to associate itself with that? Remind your administrators how many people are using Facebook actively. If you can get information about how many people are in your community's network, that could help. Show your administrator what other libraries are doing with Facebook, too. Some very effective examples:

- Charlotte Mecklenburg Library: https://www.facebook.com/cmlibrary and ImaginOn https://www.facebook.com/libraryloft
- New York Public Library: https://www.facebook.com/newyorkpubliclibrary and Teen Central @ NYPL https://www.facebook.com/teen.central

- Multnomah County Library: https://www.facebook.com/mult colib
- Carnegie Library of Pittsburgh—Teen Services: https://www.facebook.com/clpteen
- Also check out Libraries using Facebook, a group on Facebook that allows libraries to post their own pages and discuss Facebook issues: http://www.facebook.com/group.php?gid = 8408315708

And here are some excellent articles about the benefits of using social media tools to market your library:

- Virtually Yours: Online Tools Your Library Needs Now and Why: http://speakquietly.blogspot.com/2010/04/virtually-yours-online-tools-your.html. Gives great, concise, strong facts that back up the need for social media integration as well as the benefits of using these sites.
- David Lee King writes a lot about social media, including:
  - "Why do Librarians Use Facebook?" http://www.davidleeking.com/2010/01/08/why-do-librarians-use-facebook/.
  - "10 Reasons NOT to Quit Facebook," http://www.davidleeking.com/2010/05/04/10-reasons-to-not-quit-facebook/
  - "Humanizing your Facebook Pages," http://www.davidleeking.com/2010/02/09/humanizing-your-facebook-pages/
  - "Facebook Pages Basics," http://www.davidleeking.com/2009/07/08/facebook-pages-basics-a-screencast/
- Libraries in Social Networking Software: http://meredith.wolfwater.com/wordpress/2006/05/10/libraries-in-social-networking-software/. In this 2006 article, Meredith Farkas wrote an excellent overview of libraries and social media, including a huge number of resources at the end. While you may think this might be dated because it was written in 2006—it's not.

And of course, once you start using social networks to promote the library, make sure you are keeping statistics and gathering other data that will help you continue to advocate for its use. Think about reference questions that were answered online, youth participation online, and other anecdotes and comments from teens. And keep track of how many people are using your online services. As usage grows, so will your administrators' faith in the medium.

Outreach is perhaps not the most fun aspect of managing a teen program (though some librarians love it), but it's essential if you want to connect with teens. Even if you have a built-in teen audience, you shouldn't stop there. Reach out to teens who have never been in the library; they should have the chance to experience your programs and services, too. Making connections with teens is one of the most important parts of your job. It really is where everything begins: first come the teens, then comes the program. Outreach is the best way of ensuring that you're getting the teens.

NOTES

1. "Facebook," *Alexa*, March 26, 2011, available at http://www.alexa.com/siteinfo/Facebook.com.

2. Peter Corbett, "Facebook Deomgraphics and Statistics Report 2010–145$ Growth in 1 Year," *iStrategyLabs*, January 4, 2010, available at http://www.istrategylabs.com/2010/01/facebook-demographics-and-statistics-report-2010-145-growth-in-1-year/.

3. "Twitter.com," *Quantcast*, March 2011, available at http://www.quantcast.com/twitter.com.

7

BUDGET

GETTING YOUR BEARINGS

You can't do anything that costs money if you don't have the money to do it. But it's not as simple as that. It might take you a while to figure out how much money to ask for. The first time I started at a job, I asked for way too much. The second time, I asked for far too little. Both scenarios are possible given that you have no idea how much money you're going to need for your new program. Going back and forth a few times is natural until you find that perfect balance of how much you'll need to maintain your program plus develop new initiatives. And before you can even ask, you have to think about *how* to ask—how to show that your program deserves funds.

Your library has a teen program. Clearly your library values teen services. But what does that mean? What it needs to mean is that you have a designated budget, comparable to the budgets of other departments, which you can use to build your collection, programming, and services. So, before you do anything else, find out what other departments are allotted and what they spend, if you can. Teen departments serve a much smaller population than adult and children's services, simply by virtue of catering to a smaller percentage of your user base. Chances are, therefore, that you're not going to get the same budget as the reference department. However, that doesn't mean that your budget should be a tiny piece of the pie.

Talk to the finance manager, accountant, or bookkeeper, whoever deals with the day-to-day budget at your library. Find out how she keeps the books and what line items she uses. Do different budgets have different codes? Base your budget around those line items because it makes it easier for the powers that be to envision how you'll spend. Some funds might come out of budgets that you don't control—professional development, for example, or equipment. In those cases, ask how your budget requests should be presented and how you will be notified of what you've been allotted.

Ask your manager how he or she would like your budget request presented. In what format? Excel is probably the easiest way to go. How much detail is needed? And when? Some managers like to see a very granular budget, and others will accept totals for certain line items, with no breakdown. Make sure you are very clear on the process before you do anything.

WHERE WILL THE MONEY GO?

Another thing to do before you go any further is stop thinking about money for a second and start thinking about your plan. What are your goals for the year—and beyond? Where do you see your department heading over the next five years, and what will it take to get there? If you think the future is mobile, then you have to start playing around with mobile tools, which means you need a smartphone, the chance to get some professional development, a contract with a text message vendor...the list will grow. How many books do you want to add to the collection this year? Do you need some computers for the teen room? How many programs do you want to host?

There are six major areas of budget planning in any public service department:

1. Collection. This includes anything that circulates: books, DVDs, magazines, audio books, video games, equipment, and the like. Magazines are often broken out of this; find out how your library does it.

2. Programming. This includes supplies, staff hours, advertising, hiring outside instructors, prizes, and refreshments.

3. Technology, sometimes partnered with equipment. This is a broad category that can contain anything from laptops to thumb drives to software updates. Equipment could be a DVD player, a microphone for podcasting, or speakers.

4. Furniture and big ticket items. These often come out of a separate budget altogether, and I would recommend putting in these requests as sparingly as possible—but *do* ask for things, especially if you're creating a new space!

5. Databases and other online subscriptions. Sometimes these resources can be split between departments, though for simplicity's sake I usually tried not to do that.

6. Personnel. If you have staff, chances are you don't have to worry about this, but ask, just in case. You may have to talk about part-time hours and interns.

I have dealt with allocating money to different budget areas in two different ways, and I imagine these are the two most common ways for administrators to distribute funds. One is to ask for and receive a lump sum, and the other is to request specific amounts for each individual line item. If you are given a lump sum amount, you may still want to track your budget by line item, in order to be able to analyze that data later on. Budget analysis is crucial for presenting the most accurate budget request possible each year. I'll get into this more later. If you are given a line item or account-based budget, one question you might ask is whether or not money is fungible—that is, can you use funds from one account for an expense in any of the other accounts. (Put another way, can you go over your book budget as long as you leave some money in your technology budget?) The fungible budget is more focused on the total, or bottom line, than it is the individual line items (or accounts).

I do think it's wise to start with a blank slate and break your budget down on a micro level. Create a worksheet for yourself (or borrow Figure 7.8) and keep it saved every year. Depending on your administrators, you may need to present your budget in this micro detail, or you may just need to put forth the lump sums.

ADVOCATING FOR YOUR PROGRAM
Supporting Initiatives

If you're basing your budget request around your departmental goals, then you're already on the way toward justifying your requests. Not every budget item needs to be supported by a major initiative—some money goes to upkeep and basic growth. But every major initiative should be reflected in your budget request. Here's an example of how this might look for your own records:

Goals and budgetary needs for FY 2009–10

Expand graphic novel collection
  Increase number of items by 50
Develop gaming program
  Nintendo Wii
  Three games
  Monthly game tournament with prizes and snacks
Host weekly homework-help program
  School supplies
  Snacks
Increase outreach to ESOL speakers
  Increase number of Spanish-language items by 25
  Bring in part-time staff member to lead monthly discussion group

Assign monetary values to these needs and you have a justification. Figure 7.1 shows what that would look like.

Statistics

You're new, and your program is new, so you don't have any statistics. Or do you? What statistics are already being kept in the library—circulation, program attendance? Is there any way you can use these?

Circulation statistics can be captured via your ILS. These numbers can be directly tied to your collection budget requests. Areas with the highest circ deserve the most money. Areas with low circ either need to be revitalized or given a lower priority come acquisitions time. Try to figure out what the numbers mean. If your series books aren't circing, for example, is it because the most recent books haven't been purchased? Other reasons for low circulation can be missing copies, unattractive or outdated covers, the poor condition of materials. If popular titles aren't going out as much as you would like, are there too few copies on the shelf? Are you meeting the demand for holds? All of these factors should be carefully considered when analyzing circulation statistics.

Expand graphic novel collection Increase number of items by 50	50 items @ $20/item = **$1,000**
Develop gaming program Nintendo Wii Three games Monthly game tournament with prizes and snacks	$229 $120 12 events @ $40 = $480 TOTAL = **$829**
Host weekly homework-help program School supplies Snacks	52 events @ 15 = $780 52 events @ 20 = $1,040 TOTAL = **$1,820**
Increase outreach to ESOL speakers Increase number of Spanish-language items by 25 Bring in part-time staff member to lead monthly discussion group	25 items @ $20/item = $500 3 hours/month @ $12/hour = $432 TOTAL = **$932**
TOTAL	**$4,581**

Figure 7.1: Justifying your budget.

Circ stats can not only support your collection requests, they may be able to support other requests, too. Figure 7.2 contains some examples to get you thinking:

If attendance statistics already exist for adult and children's programs, mine that data. If you know, for example, that lectures and discussion groups don't do so well, but book groups are popular, you can use that as justification to build book group expenses into your programming budget. This is especially useful if the children's department has been doing programs for teens or even tweens. If nothing else, these numbers will give you a sense of community interests and they are a good jumping off point; they are also a good way to advocate for taking a risk in planning a new program for teens. If something works for one particular age group, maybe it will work for high school students, too.

Statistics work both ways—if there is a program that has traditionally taken place for teens for years, but isn't really working in terms of numbers, you can use the stats to justify a cut. That said, I am very nervous about relying too heavily on statistics, especially for teen programs, as I think successes in programming often have far more to do with the experiences of the teens than the number of teens who show up. But if you are

Statistic	Initiative
Highest circulation in the summer months	Develop a vigorous summer reading program, since that is when teens are in the library.
Lowest circulation from November to February	Initiate high-interest programming in the winter—gaming, movies, and so on—to try to promote the library during these slower months.
High circulation of manga	Hold an anime festival Bring in an artist to teach teens how to draw their own manga
High circulation of particular Dewey ranges, like sports, knitting, photography, and music	Create programs based around those subjects. Since there isn't an age breakdown here, you may have to back this up with some anecdotal information.

Figure 7.2: Program initiatives reflected in the budget request.

trying to decide which program deserves funding, statistics can be one way to justify your decision.

Anecdotal Evidence

Rather than having this evidence come from you—"I hear teens like video games!"—try having it come straight from the horses' mouths. Get a group of teens together. Any teens. Young, old, boys, girls—whoever you can grab. Explain what you're doing, and how you'd like to get their help in asking for more of something. Ask them what *they* would like to see so that they're genuinely asking for things they want, as opposed to shilling for you. Their true interest in these materials will shine through, and they will probably feel pretty good about themselves in getting involved on this level—and imagine how proud they will be if you are actually, as a result, able to purchase these materials! Use these tactics only for the biggest-ticket items. And you should also gauge how open your administrators are to these appeals. If the library tends to grant budget requests without much of a fuss, then going overboard with your proposal might not be as charming as you might think. But if there is one thing you *really* want to do, and you know it's going to be a tough sell, either because you've heard whispers of resistance or others have run up against a brick wall in the past, then consider getting the teens involved. This not only shows that you are fully committed to the budget initiative, it shows that teens would actually use or take advantage of the service or materials if the administration goes out on a limb and approves the purchase. This can make administrators feel a little less apprehensive when they shell out the cash.

Videos are easy enough to make. Using a Flip camera is the cheapest and simplest way of shooting a video, but you could also ask to borrow the library's better video camera, if one exists, and use a tripod. Videos could either be straight interviews, in which you ask teens questions and they answer (or teens could interview each other) or more elaborate scenarios. If teens want to write and perform in little skits to illustrate how much they would appreciate a certain addition to the teen program, by all means let them do it! Just make sure it's clear, easy to understand, appropriate, and not too long. Remember, you have to show this to your administrators.

Letters are the old standby, used by librarians everywhere—and used by library boards, friends groups, and directors who are trying to advocate for library services to the greater community. In this case, consider these letters as direct appeals to the library's administration. The teens should address the letter to the decision maker and keep it short and sweet. What is it that they want, and how could it improve their experience in the library? For example:

Dear Ms. Lewis,

My name is James Smith and I am a junior at Woodstock High School. I am writing this letter because I believe the Woodstock Library would greatly benefit from purchasing an Xbox 360 and some games. I love the library, and I am here all the time, but I think that more teens would use the library if they were able to play games here. I myself would play them all the time, and all of my friends would, too. I think that being able to play games in the library would make the library more appealing to other teens.

Thank you so much for considering this.

Sincerely,
James Smith

I would not dump a bushel of letters on my administrator's desk, but rather collect a sample of the best letters and hand them over, explaining that these were the three best of 35 letters, or whatever you have.

This will not only show your boss how passionate the teens are about a particular item, it will also put a human spin on your request. Again, I caution you to do this only if your request is a potentially tough sell and your administrators have expressed that they would like confirmation that a certain material or program or service will actually be taken advantage of.

Quotes are an easier way to include teen voices in your budget proposal— and perhaps a bit less dramatic than entire letters. You can ask teens to write down reasons why they would appreciate something and then cull those for meaningful quotes. Ask the teens to be creative and write from a personal perspective. These quotes could then go into any written materials that you submit along with your budget report.

Stories are written by you, not teens. Libraries and other nonprofit organizations do this all the time to promote their services, and you should borrow a page from their book. Write a story, just like you're writing a feature article, about how teens are using the library, and how they want to use the library. Interview the teens you know, as though you were doing so for a college paper or a newspaper article. Go prepared to ask questions that will lead to answers about whatever it is you're advocating for. For example, if you are trying to develop an after-school homework program, and your administrators aren't sure it's going to be used by teens who usually play sports after school:

1. When do you do your homework now?
2. Where do you do your homework now?
3. Do you feel like the library does enough to support your studying habits?
4. What challenges do you face in getting your homework done? Noise, space, time?
5. If we were to offer an after-school homework program, would you come? Would your friends? Do you think other teens would come?
6. What would you like to see offered at a program like that? Snacks, school supplies, homework help, extra time on the computers?
7. How often do you come to the library now? Would you come to the library specifically for this program? Would you tell your friends about it?

Once you have all of the answers, write up a short story about their responses, and include direct quotes. You might collect the teens' names and ages to give those reading it some context.

THE BUDGET PROPOSAL

What follows is a sample budget proposal, taking into consideration many of the factors I have discussed above. Again, this is based on my experiences in drafting budget proposals, and the requirements at your library may be different. I have often been asked to submit a request for "standard" needs and then "wish list" requests—what could the department do more of, or do better, if allocated more funds? That is incorporated in the following example.

Budget Request for FY 2009–10

Woodstock teens have already found a place for themselves in the library; now it is my job to build on those relationships and reach out to teens who have not been through our doors since childhood—or ever. To that end, I am focusing on the following goals for FY 2009–10:

- A more developed graphic novel collection
- Support of the Woodstock high and middle school
- A gaming program
- Increased after-school and weekend programming for teens

These goals are reflected in my budget request that follows.

Book budget request

Goal: Support Woodstock Middle School summer reading list

Goal: Develop popular graphic novel collection (second-highest circulating collection in the teen collection)

Gaming budget request

Goal: Develop formal gaming program, with the intention of attracting more teens to the library.

Programming budget request

Goal: Increased after-school and weekend programming to teens. As teens make up about 20 percent of our population but currently may attend only 5 percent of library programs, I wish to increase the number of programs available. In the past, writing, reading, and academic-oriented programs have been popular, but as you

Teen Services		
	Standard	Increases
Books (see below)	**14,320**	**16,320**
Audiobooks	**1,800**	**2,800**
Gaming (see below)	**3,100**	**3,950**
Programming (see below)	**10,540**	**12,615**
Database (tutor.com)	**6,500**	**6,500**
Teen Services total	**36,260**	**42,185**
Materials		
	Standard	Increases
	Bookends	Gaming chairs
	Shelf talkers	Replacement carpet squares

Figure 7.3: Proposed budget with standard and increased requests.

Action	Requested	Notes
Standard		
Summer reading	2,000	multiple copies of est. 20 titles
Building graphic novel collection	3,000	200 titles (est.)
Maintaining current collection	8,000	based on FY 2009–10 spending
Book groups	720	4 meetings with 15 copies each
Nutmeg books	600	5 copies of 10 books
Total	**14,320**	
Increases		
Additional books for collection	2,000	

Figure 7.4: Sample book budget request.

Action	Requested	Notes
Standard		
Circulating games	1,000	20 games (including ongoing replacements)
Gaming consoles	300	Xbox 360
Replacement equipment (assumed)	500	Battery packs, controllers, Rock Band drums and guitars, and so on
Replacement games (assumed)	200	
Games for programming (non-circ.)	1,000	20 games
Computer games	100	5 games
Total	**3,100**	
Increases		
10 additional circulating games	500	
5 additional programming games	250	
5 additional computer games	100	
Total	**850**	

Figure 7.5: Sample gaming budget request.

can see from the quotes below, teens are also interested in more craft, movie, and music programming.

"I love to draw and take pictures, and there isn't anywhere in Woodstock to really do that except for some classes at school. It would be amazing if the library could have some classes on this."—Morgan J., age 17

"There are a ton of bands in Woodstock, but no one ever has anywhere to play. A battle of the bands would be so popular. My friends and I would love it."—Daniel M., age 15

"I used to come into the library and do all kinds of cool things like make stuff—t-shirts and collages and stuff—and I still want to do that even though I'm not a kid anymore!"—Elyse A., age 14

Goal: Allow the newly formed Teen Advisory Board to plan three programs per year.

END OF THE YEAR ANALYSIS

It's not the best idea to just up your budget request by a certain percentage each year; rather, examine each line item and imagine you're starting from scratch again. This is particularly applicable if you're linking your budget requests to your annual plan for the department. Of course this can build off of the previous year's budget. If you stuck to the limit and were able to buy everything that you needed, then that number can be used as a baseline for the next year, plus any additional expenses.

A good way to start is to compare budget to actual expense. It's not perfect because you're probably putting in your budget request months before the end of the fiscal year, but you can project and look at general patterns.

Use the following numbers in your budget request. Figure 7.7 shows that $10,000 for the collection was probably not enough, as it's nearly all gone with several months to go in the budget cycle. Either you bought too much at the beginning of the year (and below I will discuss methods for doling out a budget over the course of the year), or you were not able to keep up with demand with the budget you had. Whichever it is, articulate this to the person in charge of the money. Again, in the previous example, $10,000 was probably just right for programming, since there is still nearly $4,000 to spend with 4 months to go. (Because programming expenses cannot be lumped together as much as programming—again, discussed below—you will know pretty clearly what's left to be spent in this scenario.) And think about these numbers in terms of advocacy—if you're not asking for an increased programming budget, maybe you could get a little more for books? Or if you're going to cut a database that gets very little use, maybe that could go toward gaming supplies?

Reviewing your expenses in this way is also a good excuse to check in at the end of the year to see what kind of trajectory you're on. Will you be over on certain items? Then slow way down. Under? Maybe get in a few last-minute purchases before the books close. Or if you're right on track—great! Which brings us to tracking expenses.

Action	Requested	Notes
Standard		
Summer reading	3,710	See below
TAB	1,200	3 major events per year
Snacks for weekly programs	1,800	3 programs per week at $15/program
Supplies for weekly programs	1,040	1 program per week requiring supplies @ $20/program
Teen writing competition	1,350	Prizes, supplies, and printing
College admissions series	240	2 per quarter (excluding summer)
Major programs (author visits, etc.)	1,200	1 per quarter (excluding summer)
Total	**10,540**	
Summer reading breakdown		
Snacks	720	24 small programs @ $25; 2 large programs @ $60
Prizes	515	1 $5 gift card, 6 $10 gift cards, 1 $300 prize, 4 $25 prizes, 1 $50 prize
Performers/instructors	1,500	3 at $500 each
Supplies	975	Supplies for 9 programs, viewing rights for movie
Subtotal	*3,710*	
Increases		
Increase after-school homework help to 2/week	875	
Additional 1 major program/season	1,200	
Total	**2,075**	

Figure 7.6: Sample programming budget request.

	Budgeted FY 2008–9	Actual as of March 2009	Requested FY 2009–10
Collection	10,000	8,535	12,000
Programming	10,000	6,220	10,000

Figure 7.7: Sample year-to-date budget totals.

Tracking Expenses

I'm sure there are many methods for tracking expenses. Over the years, the method that I have found most useful is this:

- Keep a spreadsheet on your computer with a section for each line item as they have been presented to you for your budget—books, audiobooks, games, programs, and so forth.

- Every time you get an invoice to approve, make a purchase on your corporate credit card, or get reimbursed for a purchase in one of these line items, write it down in the spreadsheet.

- Every month, ask for a report from your accountant/finance manager/other that details every expense charged to these line items over the past month.

- Compare the two amounts. Check with the finance manager on expenses that should not be attributed to your department. Add expenses that you have missed to your spreadsheet.

- Figure 7.8 is a sample expense sheet that is similar to one that I have used.

Planning Purchases

As I mentioned earlier, you will need to come up with a game plan for how you are going to spend the money allocated to your department throughout the year. It's not wise to spend money as the urge strikes you for a couple of reasons. One, many libraries like their employees to be mostly spent out by the start of the third quarter—in most cases, April 1. This means that expenses stay in the budget year in which they were allocated; in other words, expenses intended for one fiscal year will not be paid in the next. This could be a good thing for you, as it means that you will not lose money that is not spent. But it does mean that you must be cognizant of how you will spend money throughout the year.

Programming Expenses				
Expense	**Event**	**Date**	**Vendor**	**Cost**
Snacks	Anime Afternoon	12/10/09	Stop & Shop	43.10
DVD	Anime Afternoon	12/10/09	Best Buy	19.99
Prizes	New Moon Party	12/15/09	Hot Topic	32.50
Crafts	Holiday cards	12/17/09	Walmart	52.00
Misc.	Podcasting	1/7/10	Amazon.com	99.25
			TOTAL	151.55
			BUDGETED	300.00
			BALANCE	148.45

Figure 7.8: Sample expense sheet.

For example, if you receive $10,000 for books, you know that book invoices can often lag by a month—even more if processing by the vendor is involved. If you order a book in January, it might not show up at your door (with its invoice) until February or even March. So if you give yourself a date, say April 1, by which most of your book budget should be gone, then you divide up your funds to be spent out in the first three quarters of the year—in this example, about $3,300 a quarter. An even more sophisticated way of looking at it is to determine which time periods have a greater demand on purchasing. So, if you know that you'll have to buy a ton of books right after the YALSA best-of lists come out, then make sure you focus your spending that quarter around the middle of January. Otherwise, you're going to spend money you might need later on. The tricky issue, of course, is summer reading. Around the time you are purchasing your summer reading books is the time when the financial books start to inch their way closed. I would highly suggest sitting down with the finance manager to come up with a plan. If you know you are going to be ordering a mountain of books in May, is there a way of anticipating when invoices will arrive? Can you rush the orders to ensure that the invoices show up before July 1? Or should you assume that your summer reading money will always pay for the purchases you make in the previous fiscal year? It's worth talking about.

Material purchases can be front-loaded so that you will only need to buy the bare minimum—patron requests and hot new titles—as the year winds down. Programs are another story. Not all programming materials and supplies can be bought ahead of time, and speakers, authors, and instructors certainly won't invoice you until they actually show up.

SOURCES OF FUNDING

You'll get a budget every year, and that's the money you have to spend throughout the coming 12 months. Library budgets all over the country are being slashed down to their bare bones. This could be happening to you. You could be asked to make choices about what's most important in your budget. I'll talk about this more in the next section, but, for now, here are some places where you can look for additional source of funding. Be aware of what you need to speaking to your administrators about—applying for grants is usually A-OK, but you should always check before soliciting funds or undertaking a fundraiser of any kind.

Grants

Grants are financial awards given to those who undergo the often extensive process of applying for them. Grants are usually project-based, and you must typically follow up with the funding body to let them know how you spend their money.

The best place for look for grants is in the Foundation Directory, which is very expensive but might be available through your library. Another book to peruse is *The ALA Big Book of Library Grant Money* (http://www.alastore.ala.org/detail.aspx?ID=2887).

Be forewarned, though, that many of these grants are not for beginners. The process of writing a grant can be intense and time-consuming, and usually you can't just write one without knowing what you're looking for, specifically. So, it might be better to identify projects that you'd like to fund and then look for a grant to do that. Grants are not for small-scale projects, though some agencies do offer mini grants. Therefore, I would suggest thinking about broad-range initiatives. For example, if you know that you would like to create a town-wide writing program, with monthly programs, speaker series, workshops, and the creation of a bound book of teen work, then you might consider applying for a grant.

If you've never written a grant proposal before, there are a few places to start:

- YALSA offers many grant opportunities, many of which are on the (relatively) small side and many of which are for specific things, like conference attendance or research projects: http://www.ala. org/ala/mgrps/divs/yalsa/awardsandgrants/yalsaawardsgrants. cfm.

- The Institute of Museum and Library Services is a great place to search for library-specific grants, at http://www.imls.gov/appli cants/applicants.shtm. You can search by grant name, institution type, and project type. But again, you're going to find a *ton* of results. and they can be difficult to sort out.

- The Library Grants blog (http://librarygrants.blogspot.com/) is a good one to watch for announcements about grants with a library focus. The blog does a fine job of describing the grants so that you can decide whether or not they are the right ones for you.

- Scholastic gathers many grants for libraries and librarians on its website at http://www.iread2.com/librarians/programs/grants. htm. Some are one-time grants, while others are ongoing.

- Definitely visit your state library website. Most state libraries or state library consortiums offer grant opportunities. There may be one person on their staff who is responsible for administering grants and acting as a liaison with libraries, so give them a call and ask loads of questions.

Sponsorships

This, to me, is a bit more of a gray area, since it involves the library seeking out businesses that might be interested in sponsoring certain events or materials or services. There is no set process for obtaining sponsorships, as there is with applying for grants. Some libraries do not seek sponsorships as a rule, while others welcome and even seek them out.

If you are working on something that you think might be an attractive sponsorship opportunity for a businesses or individual, the first thing to do is to speak with your director. There may be reasons why he or she does not want to pursue this funding opportunity. Some libraries use sponsorships to fund a regularly occurring event, like a program series or a large annual program. If you are adding a new space or large piece of equipment to the library—a film lab, for example, or a teen reading area—then a sponsor might be the best way to get this off the ground. But that doesn't mean that a sponsorship has to involve a huge amount of money. Small businesses may be interested in sponsoring a small series of events, like providing all of the lemonade and cookies for a monthly book discussion. The main reason why this might not be possible is because libraries often rely on certain donors, corporate and otherwise, to give as much as they can to the library every year. Asking a sponsor to donate a small-ish amount might make them feel as though they do not need to donate any more than that—which can harm the fundraising efforts of the library. This is why it's so important to speak with your director about these ideas.

Fund-raisers

Chances are, your library already manages at least one fund-raiser, whether it's a charity party, a book sale, or a fund-raising drive. The best place to start is to get actively involved in these efforts. That said, the monies raised often go into the annual operating fund, which gets distributed to different area, and can't really be lobbied for. There may be a way, though, for you to raise funds directly for teen services—if, again, this is allowed by the administration. Organizing a fund-raiser can be a huge undertaking. There are a few ways to implement this that are a bit easier than others:

- Book sales. Either sell books that have been withdrawn from the collection, or partner with a local bookseller to sell new books and take a small portion of the profit for the library. This is definitely possible through chain bookstores like Barnes & Noble and Borders, and of course Scholastic Book Sales are nearly ubiquitous.
- Wish lists. Libraries are starting to create Amazon and eLibris wish lists for themselves and posting them directly on their websites. You could do this just for the teen collection. For examples of what some public libraries are doing, check out:
  - Lewes (DE) Public Library: http://www.leweslibrary.org/node/629
  - Glendale (CA) Public Library: http://library.ci.glendale.ca.us/amazon_wishlist.asp
  - Rodman (OH) Public Library: http://www.rodmanlibrary.com/rpl/libserv/amazon.html
- Read-a-thons. Just as in a walk-a-thon, teens get sponsored for the number of pages they can read, either in the library during an

event or over the course of some period of time. Here are some examples of what other libraries and schools have done:

- Horace Mann School: http://mann.spps.org/Read-a-thon.html
- Evanston (IL) Public Library: http://eplfriends.blogspot.com/p/read-thon.html
- Ellwood (PA) City Library: http://www.ellwoodcitylibrary.com/read.html

- Selling merchandise. Libraries are starting to put their logos on everything from mugs to flash drives to beanie babies, then selling those in a little store, kind of like a museum store. For a very high-end example of how this could look, check out the Los Angeles Public Library's store at http://www.lfla.org/store/. On a smaller scale, it would be easy to put items in a display case, and then offer them for sale, either through the circulation desk or the computer lab. It's relatively simply to put your logo on stuff, either through Café Press or Zazzle.

BUDGET CHALLENGES

More than any other area, budget challenges affect everything that you do, because not having enough money means that you have to make cuts from everywhere—services, staffing, materials, and programs. If your library, like so many other libraries, is facing budget cuts, here are some ways of handling it.

Not Getting Enough

You will never get enough. Even if you get a lot, it will never be enough. Once you come to terms with that, you will start to learn how to make the most of what you get. But even if it's never enough, sometimes it's really, *really* not enough. These are the times when the entire library's budget is being reduced, and everyone is feeling the pain. In those cases, your administrators will ask you to develop a budget that reflects the bare necessities. You can, certainly, think about undertaking one of the fundraising methods discussed above, but you will also have to make some hard choices about how you're going to spend the little money you have. In this situation, take the time to really analyze what you're providing and how you can prioritize.

Worthington (Ohio) Libraries did a great job of reaching out to its teens when faced with budget cuts in 2009. Read their blog post here, and make sure to click to the survey that they created: http://www2.worthington libraries.org/teen/blog/index.cfm?commentID=362. If you know that you will be faced with budget cuts in the coming year, definitely reach out to teens to get their input on what matters most to them. Surveys work well, as do focus groups. Post polls on your Facebook page and leave paper surveys lying around. Not only does this raise awareness of the budgetary issues at hand, it gives teens a voice.

Now look at the materials that you provide. Which ones are essential? Materials in general are essential, but how many can you get away with providing? Can you reduce the number of books and other materials that you purchase? Can you eliminate purchasing multiple copies, or would you prefer to keep multiples of super-popular titles and cut out the fringe books that don't really get checked out? Doing a circ survey would be a good idea at this point, to get a sense of which materials would be most missed were they no longer provided.

Programs can be cut. Which ones are the best attended—by that I mean the most consistently and with the most attendees? Which have the most loyal followings? And which new programs do you feel there is a distinct need for? Can you justify that, either with statistics or some other data? Which programs can be done for free or for very little money? If you can cut an extremely expensive program in order to provide many more cheap programs, then do it. And how can you reduce costs? If you are purchasing books for every kid who comes to a book discussion, maybe it's time to look at interlibrary loaning them. If you always provide supplies for free, maybe teens could provide their own white t-shirt to decorate. Along these lines, you could reduce the amount of prizes given out or the value of those prizes. Teens will understand.

Because this is such a common challenge in libraries, you will find many resources available to help you navigate the world of budget limitations:

- YALSA's Recession Relief Resources: http://wikis.ala.org/yalsa/ index.php/Recession_Relief_Resources. Free stuff, funding opportunities, and more.
- The YALSA blog's "economy" tag: http://yalsa.ala.org/blog/ category/economy/. This includes the series "31 Days of Dollars and Sense," a month-long series on posts in December 2009: http://yalsa.ala.org/blog/tag/31-days-of-dollars-and-sense/.
- ALA's Advocating in a Tough Economy Toolkit: http://www.ala. org/ala/issuesadvocacy/advocacy/advocacyuniversity/toolkit/ is full of good tips for promoting library services in an economic

downturn. And visit ALA's Budgeting and Finance wiki at http:// wikis.ala.org/professionaltips/index.php/Budgeting_and_ Finance.

- Visit your state library website for resources. People are there to help you.

Managing your budget can be one of the hardest things you have to do as a librarian. It's scary and daunting. If you make a mistake, it can be problematic to fix. Library budgets are so tight that there often isn't any room for error. For all of those reasons, you need to start being conscientious about your budget from the start. Have numerous conversations with your manager and your library's bookkeeper. Ask your colleagues if you can see what systems work for them. And keep track! As soon as you spend a dime, record it on your expense sheet and tuck the receipt away in a place you'll remember. The best way to be a responsible and successful budget manager is to stay on top of it.

8

◇ ◇ ◇

PROFESSIONAL DEVELOPMENT

You're building a teen program from the ground up—right? Well, gee, that sounds pretty hard. Maybe you're a rock star who can do it all on his or her own. Check that: you *are* a rock star. But no one can do everything on their own. It's OK to ask for help; to solicit the advice of others; to teach yourself new things; and to always, always, always keep learning. This chapter addresses professional development in its many forms— networking, building up your résumé, and continuing education. You have joined a field with a seemingly endless amount of opportunities for all of these things, both in person, virtually, or some combination thereof. And of course, there's the money issue—so I'll get to that, too.

LIBRARY ORGANIZATIONS

If nothing else, librarians are exceptionally good at networking and gathering together. This is especially helpful in a field in which you are sometimes the only librarian in the building—which is the case with many school librarians—or, more often, the only teen librarian. You can easily find opportunities to continue educating yourself in teen services, which is excellent given that teen librarians must stay current in order to stay viable.

The American Library Association (ALA) is the largest and best-known organization for librarians and the first place you should look for professional development opportunities. ALA is large, and therefore can be difficult to navigate, but no one should be intimidated by it. It's easiest to get involved with ALA if you know someone who's involved, but it's also possible to dive in on your own.

ALA, as you may know, is made up of many divisions. The two that you will likely find most useful and interesting are the Young Adult Library Services Association (YALSA) and the American Association of School Librarians (AASL). The Association of Library Services for Children (ALSC), which serves children up to age 14, could be of interest to you if you serve middle school students, but it is really a resource for children's librarians and will only address the youngest of your users. You may also find ALA's roundtables to be of interest—the New Members Roundtable is one that all new members are automatically enrolled in. The NMRT holds events at conferences and has information online for members (see the next section for information on online resources).

You may be interested in joining other, non–youth services oriented ALA divisions. The Library and Information Technology Association, or LITA, has members from all kinds of libraries. According to LITA's website, "the membership includes new professionals, systems librarians, library administrators, library schools, vendors and anyone else interested in leading edge technology and applications for librarians and information providers. Programs are offered for everyone from absolute beginners to hi-tech professionals." LITA hosts some great events at ALA conferences, including Top Tech Trends, where librarian trend spotters highlight popular and upcoming innovations. The Public Library Association, or PLA, obviously only applies to those working in public libraries, but it addresses a broad range of issues relating to that arena, including management, advocacy, and programming, among other issues of interest to teen librarians.

State organizations are another place to get started. Search the Web for the name of your state and the words *library association,* and you will find what you're looking for. State associations often host their own annual conferences, provide professional development opportunities, and offer grants opportunities, among other resources. There are also state school library associations for school librarians, as well as for public librarians who want to be more involved and well-rounded.

Local associations can be a wealth of information and resources. Because they are smaller than national and state organizations, they are not always obvious to new librarians. A good place to start would be to ask your colleagues if any consortiums or regional organizations exist in your area. Or, call the state library—they will be able to fill you in. Note that the state library is often different from the state library association. In Connecticut, there is the Connecticut Library Association, the Connecticut State Library, and the numerous roundtables for librarians that meet in different regions of the state based on service areas—young adults, children, technical services, interlibrary loan, and so on. In Massachusetts, it's even more complicated. There is a commonwealth library, the Massachusetts Library Association, the Massachusetts Board of Library Commissioners, and the five regional library systems.

Your library school will remain an excellent resource to you even after you have left. Visit the school's website to find career information, networking contacts, and continuing education opportunities. Some schools offer mentoring programs, which can be especially useful for school librarians or public librarians who are in small organizations or are the only teen librarian in the building.

ONLINE RESOURCES

Professional development often costs money, which in this day and age can be hard to come by. Fortunately, there are free resources to be had online. For access to some, you must join an organization, which is an annual expense. For others, the resources are there for the taking.

Websites, Wikis, and More

YALSA, among other things, offers numerous professional development resources on its website, all of them free to members and non-members alike. Some of note:

- Booklists and book awards: http://www.ala.org/ala/mgrps/divs/ yalsa/booklistsawards/booklistsbook.cfm. These lists are great for readers' advisory and collection development. My favorites are Popular Paperbacks for Young Adults, which are grouped subject, and Quick Picks for Reluctant Young Adult Readers, which contain both fiction and nonfiction books that are great for readers of all levels.

- Teen Read Week: http://www.ala.org/ala/mgrps/divs/yalsa/ teenreading/trw/trw2010/home.cfm. This annual event draws awareness to teen literacy and helps promote library services to young adults. It takes place every October. The TRW site on YALSA is a place to find ideas for programming at any time of year. The TRW wiki (http://wikis.ala.org/yalsa/index.php/Teen_Read_Week) is a repository of ideas for current and past Teen Read Weeks and is full of booklists, contest ideas, and sample programs.

- YALSA Wiki: http://wikis.ala.org/yalsa. This is the main wiki for YALSA, of which the TRW wiki is an offshoot. There are too many resources here to list, but it's worth taking a look to get your bearings on how the organization works.

Other places to look online for professional development opportunities:

- *Booklist*, the review journal of ALA, offers webinars on specific genres, trends in publishing, and services—not just for teen librarians. Visit http://www.booklistonline.com.

- State library organizations often offer webinars, webcasts, and discussion groups, including LISTSERVs. Check your state library's website, but also check the library associations and organizations of other states, since these opportunities are open to all, not just state residents.

- WebJunction offers numerous online learning opportunities, most for a small fee, at http://www.webjunction.org/catalog. There are currently two about young adult services, but many of the non-teen courses will be applicable, too.

- ALA has a Vimeo channel with many archived webinars at http://vimeo.com/user3149093.

- The Library Professional Development Blog (http://libprofdev.wordpress.com/) posts regularly on opportunities both online and in person.

- The Search Institute has many excellent webinars on the developmental assets here: http://vimeo.com/user3149093.

- Learning Times sometimes hosts online conferences, like Innovation for Libraries in the 21st Century, co-sponsored by Alliance Library System: http://www.learningtimes.net/innovation/.

Library Websites

There are so many excellent library programs and fabulous librarians in the world that it would be impossible to list them all. I will, therefore, not pretend that this is a best of the best, or even an exclusive list, but merely a list of libraries (and some librarians) that I personally look to for inspiration and ideas. The more involved you get with conferences and social media, the more people you will meet who can be your inspirations. If your library can afford it, it can be a wonderful experience to travel to these libraries. Spend some time talking with librarians and teens, if possible. Take photographs (if you are allowed to do so—check with the librarian first). Ask for a tour and check out what's on the shelf. Even if you can't visit the *fabulous* places that everyone knows about, look to local libraries for in-person advice. Check local websites to see which libraries have teen programs, and at the very least give them a call to see if you can stop by. Programs that might not get written up in *School Library Journal* are still doing fantastic things that you can borrow and modify for your own program.

- *The Public Library of Charlotte and Mecklenberg County* (http://www.plcmc.org/) is the home of ImaginOn, the amazing theater/library hybrid in the heart of Charlotte, North Carolina. The teen space there, The Loft, can take advantage of a technology classroom, a movie studio, and a music studio. The entire PLCMC system boasts an incredible lineup of programs for teens—you will find many excellent ideas by visiting their website. When I was planning a new teen space, I visited ImaginOn and was totally blown away by the number of teens using the library to make music and movies, do crafts, and just hang out with the teen librarians. They're an excellent model for how teens can feel completely comfortable and at home in a teen space. PLCMC is on Twitter at @cmlibrary and has a popular Facebook page at http://www.facebook.com/cmlibrary.

- *Maricopa County Library* (http://www.mcldaz.org/) does an amazing job of getting teens involved in the library and the community. The Teen Leadership Experience is particularly exciting. Teens sign up at the library to volunteer at local organizations. They undergo an orientation and then must complete a certain number of hours of work in two of three areas of Maricopa County's agencies: government, community, and environment. This might include Teen Court, Head Start, the Parks department, and alternative energy plants, and, of course, the library. Additionally, teens had a large part in designing the library's Teen Oasis area, as well as involving teens in creating content for the library website. Follow Maricopa Teen Services on Twitter at @mcldteens.

- *The Hennepin County Library* (http://www.hclib.org/teens/) has a dynamic website that reflects how much it does for teens. The different branches boast an impressive number of programs, including Friday Field Trips, a program that takes teens off-site to do community service projects, outdoor activities, and visit local attractions. The site also has a section called Teens Speak, where teens post about whatever they want and comment on each other's posts. Hennepin is on a multitude of social networking sites and can be followed on Twitter at @hclib.

- *The Princeton Library* (http://www.princeton.lib.nj.us/teens/index.html) has a slick website full of content for teens. The Princeton Student Film and Video Contest is particularly impressive. The contest has been happening for seven years and is open to both high school and college students. The films are shown in a two-night screening event. Princeton also has a vibrant volunteer program, a whole host of online resources for teens, and a full schedule of programs, including two clubs—the Go Between Club for teens in grades six and seven, and the Teen Advisory Board.

- *The Kalamazoo Public Library* (http://www.kpl.gov/teens/) has a frequently updated blog for teens and a great "meet the teen staff" section. KPL host many events for teens, and hosts one of 15 of YALSA's YA Galley programs, which is called The Galley Group. The group reads new books and writes reviews of them online. KPL often brings in teen authors to meet their readers, hosts a J-Pop club that reads anime and watches manga (and eats Pocky), hosts a Young Filmmaker Festival that is in its seventh year, and runs a series of workshops about technology, called Your Digital Life.

Blogs

You should not just be reading the blogs and Twitter feeds of those who are working in teen services. Reading the thoughts of those who work in all areas of librarianship will not only inspire you in your work with teens, it will make you more well-rounded and intellectually curious. While I tend to eschew the cult of personality that surrounds many of the library world's best known thinkers and writers, it is important to keep up, whenever possible, on the theories and trends that are being discussed by these people in the profession. I also think it's a good idea to take ideas that may have been generated for non-teen service and apply them to teen services in a new and exciting way. Not all of the good ideas will come from teen librarians, though there are some amazing people out there.

I recommend using Google Reader or Bloglines or a similar blog aggregator to keep up with all of your online subscriptions. I prefer Google Reader simply because I use Google for just about everything, and I like how you can share posts and other pieces of information with your friends. Both services allow you to create categories to keep all of your RSS feeds separate, which I find useful since there are a few sites I follow that are personal. Google Reader lets you set different privacy rules for each subscription or each category. You can also subscribe to RSS feeds of particular Google blog searches, such as the name of your library, the words *teen services*, your own name, and the like. Do this by completing a search in Google's blog search (http://blogsearch.google.com) and then clicking on the RSS feed icon that pops up in the address bar. If you scroll down to the bottom of the page, you can also click on "create an e-mail alert for '[search term].'" This feature will send you an e-mail every time that term occurs in a blog.

- The *YALSA* blog (http://yalsa.ala.org/blog/) is a fantastic resource that is contributed to by a large and varied number of librarians.Writers blog about a wide variety of topics, everything from graphic novels to YALSA official business to summer reading to advocacy to quirky, funny, and interesting teen services issues. While I imagine diving into the blog can be a bit daunting, I recommend using the tags to sort through the information.
- *Youth Services Corner* (http://www.youthservicescorner.com) is a blog authored by Whitney Winn, a 2008 MLIS graduate who collects resources for librarians who work with tweens and teens. She blogs about everything from traditional YA librarian issues, like book challenges, to pop culture, listing, for example, books that have been turned into current movies.
- *Pop Goes the Library* (http://www.popgoesthelibrary.com/) is a joint blog. The contributors are Sophie Brookover, Liz Burns, Melissa Rabey, Susan Quinn, John Klima, Carlie Webber, Karen Corday, and Eli Neiburger, who call themselves "pop culture librarians." As the blog's description says, "We're public, school, and academic librarians. We believe libraries can learn from and use Pop Culture to improve their collections, services, and public image. We love TV, music, the movies, comic books, anime, magazines, sports, tech, and oh yeah: reading!" From Pop Goes the Library, you will find some of the author's individual blogs: Burns's is *A Chair, a Fireplace, and a Tea Cozy* http://yzocaet.blogspot.com/; Rabey's is *Librarian by Day* http://librarianbyday.blogspot.com/; and Webber's is *Librarilly Blonde* http://librarillyblonde.blogspot.

com/. PGTL has been around since 2004 and offers insightful and thought-provoking posts about the future of libraries, trends in library services, and, of course, pop culture.

- The blog *In the Library with the Lead Pipe* (http://www.intheli brarywiththeleadpipe.org/) is not specifically for teen services librarians, though it addresses issues that will be of interest to you, including information literacy, technology, marketing, and management. The librarians who write for it are in different areas of librarianship and each address issues from a different standpoint. The blog contains articles, links to news items of interest, conference information, and theories. One of my favorite posts is by my friend Robyn Vittek, the Assistant Youth Services Coordinator for Akron-Summit County Public Library, about Teen Tech Week: http://www.inthelibrarywiththeleadpipe.org/2010/teen-tech-week-create-share-learn-your-library/.

- *The Shifted Librarian* (http://theshiftedlibrarian.com/) is Jenny Levine, who is also ALA's Internet development specialist and strategy guide. Levine writes a lot about technology issues, as you might expect, but she also has very insightful things to say about gaming in libraries, which is a particular interest of hers.

- Aaron Schmidt is the digital initiatives librarian for the District of Columbia Public Library. His blog, *Walking Paper* (http://www.walkingpaper.org/), tends to highlight snippets of information gleaned online and theorize about how they might be applied to libraries. He has also visited other libraries, many of them international, and likes to bring to light the innovations of those organizations.

- Finally, Michael Stephens is considered one of the foremost thinkers in library science. A professor at Dominican University, Stephens's blog, *Tame the Web* (http://tametheweb.com/), is a go-to site for the latest on library news, new ideas, and highlights of what everyone in libraries is (or should be) talking about. Several librarians contribute to *Tame the Web*, including Justin Hoenke, teen librarian at the Portland (ME) Public Library, who is a founding member of 8bitlibrary.com, a website for librarians, teachers, gamers, and information professionals (http://blog.8bitlibrary.com).

On a fun note, some YA authors' blogs are wonderful and funny, and you can often find out information about contests, book tours, and new titles by reading their stuff. Many YA authors now have Twitter accounts, too. Click here for a pretty comprehensive list: http://bloggingya.blogspot.

com/2009/05/authors-of-twitter.html. Some of my favorite blogs include:

- E. Lockhart (*The Boyfriend List, The Disreputable History of Frankie Landau-Banks*): http://www.theboyfriendlist.com/e_lockhart_blog/
- John Green (*Looking for Alaska, Paper Towns*): http://www.sparks flyup.com/weblog.php
- Libba Bray (the *Gemma Doyle* trilogy, *Going Bovine*): http://libba bray.livejournal.com/
- Maureen Johnson (*Thirteen Little Blue Envelopes*, the *Suite Scarlett* series): http://maureenjohnson.blogspot.com/
- Meg Cabot (a million super-popular books!): http://www.meg cabot.com/
- Sarah Dessen (*Someone Like You, Lock and Key*): http://writergrl. livejournal.com/
- Scott Westerfeld (the *Uglies* series, the *Leviathan* series): http:// scottwesterfeld.com/blog

LISTSERVs

LISTSERVs are a mixed bag. These e-mail subscription lists can be an excellent way to reach out to your fellow teen and school librarians, but they can also be an overwhelming rush of information in your inbox each day. There are some ways to avoid overload: if you can filter your e-mail, have your LISTSERV messages go directly into other folders. Some LIST-SERVs offer digests, which are daily—or even weekly—messages containing all of the e-mails sent out within that time frame. Of all the LISTSERVs available to librarians, here are the ones I think are of the most value:

- LM_NET (http://www.eduref.org/lm_net/) is a discussion group for school librarians. Subscribers can receive dozens of messages each day, on everything from tech tips to cataloging questions to requests for help identifying books.
- YALSA-BK (http://lists.ala.org/wws/info/yalsa-bk) is the most popular of the YALSA LISTSERVs. It is mostly about books, as the name implies, but it can also be a place to ask questions about booktalking, book trailers, and other book-centric programming, as well as censorship and collection development issues.

- YALSA-YAAC (http://lists.ala.org/wws/info/ya-yaac) is less popular than YALSA-BK but is subscribed to by over 1,500 members, who offer and ask questions about teen advisory boards, programming, technology, gaming, and professional development. YALSA leadership post to this LISTSERVs with information about opportunities from ALA and YALSA—grants, prizes, and the like.

Social Media

Librarians love social media. It's funny, there have been many articles written about how teens don't use Twitter (more on this in the Twitter section below), but librarians have completely, totally embraced the microblogging site and use it not just to socialize, but to get and share ideas, report back to their colleagues about conferences, ask questions of the hive mind, and post links to blogs, articles, and other items of interest. Similarly, librarians are some of the first to try new social media sites, like Foursquare and FriendFeed—now not so new—and focus a lot of their energy on getting comfortable with these media so that they can instruct their patrons on their use and also determine whether there are library applications for these sites.

Teen librarians should be especially comfortable and familiar with social media, since teens actually use it a lot. However, teens tend to be more focused on one or two sites, which surprisingly do not change that frequently. Additionally, teen librarians should see social networks as a means toward quickly and efficiently expanding one's intellectual reach, as well as staying on top of the ever-changing trend landscape.

ALA Connect (connect.ala.org) is the American Library Association's own social network. Once you join, all of the groups with which you are affiliated are tied to your profile—so, for example, you might belong to YALSA, a committee, and an interest group; all of these will be present in your profile, and all have their own space within ALA Connect for members to interact with each other. You can also join nonofficial groups that are of interest to you. There are several communication tools available via Connect. The best, I think, is the chat feature. YALSA offers frequent chat discussions of various issues, and along with other divisions, you can find webinars on a variety of topics. Anyone can join ALA Connect, but only ALA members may read certain sections of the site and post.

Twitter is a great place to connect with other librarians from many different fields. Check out Just Tweet It's directory of librarians who tweet at http://justtweetit.com/education/librarians/. This is a self-selected list. Librarians Matter, the blog of Kathryn Greenhill, listed the top 10 twittering librarians in 2008: http://librariansmatter.com/blog/2008/07/01/top-ten-twittering-librarians/. While they might not still be the top 10, these librarians are good people to follow, and the people *they* follow might be of interest to you. And finally, there is Twellow's *librarian* category at http://www.twellow.com/category_users/cat_id/346. To learn more about why Twitter is a great tool for librarians, read:

- "Twittering Libraries" (http://lis5313.ci.fsu.edu/wiki/index.php/Twittering_Libraries), a research paper by Lindy Brown.
- "Twitter for Librarians: The Ultimate Guide" (http://www.collegeathome.com/blog/2008/05/27/twitter-for-librarians-the-ultimate-guide/), an article written for College @ Home.
- "Twitter for Librarians, or 10 Ways to Use Twitter" (http://www.davidleeking.com/2007/03/10/twtter-explained-for-librarians-or-10-ways-to-use-twitter/) by David Lee King, from his blog.

Facebook has already been discussed at great length as an outreach tool, but it's a professional tool for you, too. I have noticed a trend where librarians who get to know each other via Twitter begin to friend one another on Facebook. And, lately, Facebook has become a place to find invitations to different library events, as well as a place to chat with other librarians on an informal basis. There's more:

- Hottest Facebook Groups for Librarians (http://oedb.org/blogs/ilibrarian/2007/hottest-facebook-groups-for-librarians/) was written in 2007, so buyer beware, though on cursory glance, most of these groups have grown significantly since this list was published.
- YALSA is on Facebook at https://www.facebook.com/yalsa, and a great example of how librarians are using Facebook to socialize in real life is this event, the ALA 2010 Dance Party: https://www.facebook.com/event.php?eid=191826097521352
- *Ning* is a platform that allows users to create their own social networks. Many have sprung up that relate to libraries. You need to have a Ning account in order to join these groups. There, you will find resources and discussion forums, as well as smaller groups within the Ning, such as the "Twitter as a Tool" group in Library 2.0.
- Library 2.0: http://www.library20.org/
- TeacherLibrarianNing: http://teacherlibrarian.ning.com/
- Classroom 2.0: http://www.classroom20.com/

- FriendFeed (http://friendfeed.com/) aggregates all of your social networks, from Twitter to LibraryThing to Flickr to Pandora and more. It allows you to publish a stream of information about yourself and all of your networks, as well as follow the updates of your friends.

CONTINUING EDUCATION

You don't stop learning once you get a good job. You might need to take some time off from continuing your education while you get your bearings. But even those who are wholly occupied by full-time jobs will also likely feel a desire to keep learning and to keep up on what's new. This is wise, not just because it will help you be better at your current job, but because it will help you build your résumé if you ever find yourself in a position where you wish to get a new job. And, let's face it, that will probably happen eventually, even if you stay at your library. You will move up through the organization, which will require certain skills. Or, you will move to a new area and a new library. Your on-the-job training will serve you well in both situations, but I would posit that a demonstrated interest in learning new skills and staying up-to-date on all the latest in library services will make you a more desirable candidate to search committees, et al.

Taking time out of your day for continuing education is extremely difficult, especially when you have desk hours, which you likely do. And I can't recommend that you spend personal time on such things, unless you have the time and desire to do so. We all need a healthy work–life balance, after all. If you can reserve even one hour a week to spend on your continuing education, then you will be in good shape. One hour every two weeks or every month works, too—but the more time you can devote, the better. The term *continuing education* means many things: reading articles, attending workshops and lectures, watching webinars, taking classes, and so on. Obviously, some of these things are more time consuming that others, so choose wisely based on your circumstances. If you can get time off (and be paid) to attend off-site training, great! Otherwise, stick to remote learning opportunities. In the following discussion, I'll give you my advice on where you can find such opportunities.

Make sure to write down everything you do as a teen librarian. It's important to have this information, not only in case of a job search but also for your performance evaluations. If you write regular reports to your supervisor, make sure your recent accomplishments are included. And, whenever you can, try to take something away from what you've learned and apply it to your library and the teen program. Continuing education can simply be food for thought and a chance to expand your horizons and exercise your brain, but it can also be a jump-start for a new initiative, and that's when things really get exciting. So now, here's where to look.

Library Schools

Visit your graduate school's website. Mine, Simmons, has a whole section on continuing education at http://www.simmons.edu/gslis/careers/continuing-education/. These classes are open to anyone, not just Simmons graduates. Here's a selection of what other graduate schools (selected at random) offer:

- Rutgers: http://mypds.rutgers.edu
- The University of Wisconsin: http://www.slis.wisc.edu/continueed.htm
- Southern Connecticut State University: http://www.southernct.edu/ils/programs/continuingeducation
- San Jose State University: http://slisweb.sjsu.edu/classes/nealschuman.htm
- The Catholic University of America: http://slis.cua.edu/admissions/continuinged.cfm

Even if it's not easy to see if your alma mater offers anything, it would be worth reaching out to former professors to see whether or not they can suggest anything—online classes, webinars, or even informal unconferences or discussion groups in your area. Unconferences are informal gatherings where professionals meet and decide on-site what topics they would like to explore. This might include breaking the group up into discussion groups, or asking participants to volunteer to lead on-the-fly workshops.

ALA

The American Library Association has a whole section on its website devoted to online learning at http://ala.org/ala/onlinelearning. From there, you can find learning opportunities in these major areas: collections management; issues and advocacy; management issues for library leaders; school libraries; and service delivery in libraries. Additionally, the site lists continuing education opportunities offered by ALA's numerous divisions, including YALSA and AASL, the biggies as far as teen librarians are concerned. These learning opportunities include webinars and online courses, and they usually cost money to attend. However, you can sometimes hear about free webinars or e-chats through ALA Connect.

ALA Learning, the Learning Roundtable, has been especially active as of late, with a revamped site and a blog authored by some of the field's brightest stars. The site, http://alalearning.org, is mostly a repository for information of interest and use to library professionals. Authors highlight new technologies, tips on enhancing your résumé, calls for presenters and proposals, and news about training opportunities, among other topics. The Learning Roundtable sponsors discussion groups at ALA conferences where you can gather with other librarians to talk about staff development. Remember that ALA Learning is for librarians in all fields, certainly not only teen librarians, though the best way to expand your horizons in continuing education is not to limit yourself to resources just for those in teen services.

ALA Techsource is a good blog to add to your feed reader (http://www.alatechsource.org). It's got frequent posts on library technology and consumer technology that can be applied to libraries. You can sign up for the Smart Libraries newsletter and purchase ALA's Library Technology Reports, which are in-depth publications targeting a specific area of library tech. About six reports are published a year, and many of them, though none are specifically about teen services, will be of interest to you. The same can be said for the blog posts—none of them are written for a teen librarian audience, but technology should always be of interest to teen librarians.

State Libraries and Library Associations

Your state library may be experiencing budget cuts, but it's still worth checking out their website to see whether they offer any professional development resources—webinars, meetings, courses, and so forth. Many state libraries organize small discussion or interest groups throughout the state (though this may depend on the size of your state) that can be very informative and a great networking opportunity. At the same time, see what your state library association can offer. Sometimes, starting on the state level can be a way to ease into involvement in outside professional activities. If you are interested in pitching continuing education classes or online learning opportunities, start with your state library and state library association because doing so can be amazing for your résumé. Your state library association may also organize continuing education opportunities, and, of course, they probably host an annual conference—I'll talk about that more later on in this section.

Industry Publishers and Vendors

Organizations that create and sell library products will often offer free online resources for librarians—they are a great marketing tool for the company. So take advantage of them! The question is, how do you find out about these resources if they aren't to be found in all the usual places? Well, subscribing to LISTSERVs is a good way to start, as publishers and vendors will often promote their classes this way. Subscribe not only to the national-level LISTSERVs, but also your state-level ones. And visit the sites below to see if you can sign up for more information on continuing education opportunities. Even if you can't attend a webinar, sign up so that you can find out about upcoming ones; additionally, webinars are often archived for later viewing.

OCLC not only offers not only online classes on its own products but also has partnered with *Library Journal* to offer online symposiums. Visit OCLC's News and Events Page at http://www.oclc.org/news for press releases about upcoming online learning opportunities—you can subscribe to an RSS feed of this news or sign up for e-mail updates.

Library Journal keeps an extensive list of webcasts on its website at http://www.libraryjournal.com/webcasts. These are sponsored by different publishers or vendors and can cover anything from e-books to genre fiction to new databases.

Webjunction webinars (http://www.webjunction.org/events/webinars) are live and feature specific, practical topics like fund-raising, digital preservation, and employment issues.

Booklist webinars focus on—no surprise—books, but can often link them to other areas of interest like programming, outreach, and reference. Like all of the others listed here, Booklist webinars are for librarians who serve all age groups, though there is usually something of interest to teen librarians, whether explicitly marketed that way or otherwise: http://www.booklistonline.com/GeneralInfo.aspx?id=63.

CONFERENCES

As I write this, I know how difficult it is to attend conferences. Many libraries have had to cut funding for conferences, meaning that librarians have to either not go or pay for their travel and registration out of pocket, which is certainly not an option for many people. Some librarians even need to take vacation time to go. If you truly cannot travel to attend conferences, then you must take advantage of some of the opportunities I listed previously in this section—online education, virtual meetings, and so on. But even if your library can send you to conferences, you will still have to pick and choose which you want to attend, since you won't be able to go to all of them. There are many traditional library conferences that you can choose from, but increasing numbers of librarians are attending what I will call nontraditional conferences—that is, conferences that are not geared specifically to librarians.

Traditional (Library)

There are so many traditional conferences to attend that it can be hard to keep them all straight and decide which ones are most valuable. Speak with your colleagues to get their opinions, ask your fellow teen librarians in other libraries, and definitely ask your boss.

ALA Annual takes place at the end of June in a rotating location. It is the bigger of the two ALA annual conferences; the other one is Midwinter, which takes place every January in another location. Librarians go to Annual to attend committee and board meetings, meet with vendors, and attend professional development sessions. There are very few sessions like this at Midwinter, which is ALA's business meeting—as with Annual, committees, boards, and ALA leadership all meet, and there is an exhibit hall where you can meet with vendors and see previews of new products. If you join an ALA committee or get involved in any way, you may have to attend both Annual and Midwinter, though more committees are allowing for virtual membership—that is, you do not have to attend these meetings at the conferences themselves, but rather can keep in touch with other committee members via online means. If you are interested in attending a conference for professional development purposes, you should really only consider ALA Annual, though YALSA has begun offering a pre-conference all-day institute before both conferences, which can definitely be worth attending (though it will cost you an additional fee). At Annual, you will find an almost countless amount of opportunities to learn, network, and connect. Midwinter is more a time for networking and developing your presence in ALA, if you are interested in such things.

The Public Library Association, or PLA, holds an annual conference as well. I have never attended a PLA conference, but I know many teen librarians who have. If you work with teens in a public library, you will find many useful resources at PLA. At the 2010 conference, there was a full day pre-conference about teen advocacy, a booktalking boot camp, programs on gaming, and more. By the same token, the American Association of School Librarians (AASL) also offers an annual conference with offerings not just for school librarians but for any librarians who work with youth. Both AASL and PLA sponsor events at ALA Annual and Midwinter as well.

The annual YALSA Symposium on Young Adult Literature is a new conference that takes place every November in a different location every year. This is YALSA's only conference, and I think it is definitely worth considering attending. While nominally the conference is about literature, there are many offerings on other topics, like technology, programming, outreach, and more. Attend the Symposium for continuing education first, but you will find numerous opportunities to meet new librarians and connect with YALSA leadership. This is also an opportunity to meet young adult librarians whose libraries you might be able to visit.

State and regional conferences may be an excellent option for you if you need to save money, can't travel far, or want to connect more with other librarians in your area. State conferences can have *excellent* speakers from all over the country, and both regional and national companies will be represented in the exhibit hall (though I must say that I have seen a trend over the past few years—a decline in the number of vendors who attend conferences and who can give away materials to librarians). Like with other continuing education opportunities, state library conferences can be a great place to start if you are interested in building your résumé through presenting. And you may get information that is more targeted to your region than you would at a national conference. However, not all state library conferences will be able to offer a lot on teen services due to scheduling and budgetary restrictions—in that case, your better bet may be to attend your state school library association. If you can, take a look at the offerings for each. Of course, school library conferences will be for school librarians, but they will also offer courses on collections, programs, outreach, and challenges for all librarians.

Computers in Libraries is sponsored by Information Today and takes place every March in Arlington, VA. In my experience, there is an overlap between who attends ALA conferences and who attends CiL, though you will see far fewer youth services librarians at CiL, simply because there are so few programs specifically tailored toward librarians who work with children and teens. That does appear to be changing, however, as more youth librarians get involved in integrating cutting-edge technology into their services. CiL, unlike ALA, tends to have more non-librarian presentations and speakers, and is also far less book-centric, as you can imagine. At CiL, you will be able to learn about trends that are happening that very moment, both in technology and librarianship, and you will be able to apply much of what you learn, whether it is intended for teen librarians or not, to your services to teens.

Internet Librarian is another Information Today conference, this one taking place in northern California every October. Like Computers in Libraries, sessions are not focused just on libraries but on educational technology, social media, new private sector products, and the like. Again, you might not find much specifically for librarians who work with teens, but you will likely come away inspired by what you learn. I recommend looking into courses for academic librarians, as they can often contain surprising pieces of information and advice that can be applied to your work with teens—because part of your job is to supplement the learning process that they experience through their schooling, and because the age difference between college students and high school students is not that great, you may learn about new ways of reaching teens and exposing them to new methods of learning.

Nontraditional Conferences and Conventions

Book Expo America is an annual book publishing convention. There are programs available, but the main reason to attend BEA is to meet with publishers, preview new books, and speak with authors. The convention is usually held in New York City, and you can go for the day or for the whole shebang—usually three days. Different publishers will hold events, like author lunches or panel presentations by authors or editors, and there are signing booths where different authors sit each hour. You can stand in line to have a book signed (often an advance reading copy) and chat with the author—if they are touring to promote their new book, they may be interested in visiting your library. Bring business cards and try to connect with the author in some way—it can be intimidating to speak with authors, especially if they are well-known, but authors are people, too, and many of them would be happy to visit libraries, especially those near other locations on their tour.

ComicCon takes place in two locations: in New York in October and in California in July. Like BEA, ComicCon is more of a convention than a conference—there are events, such as speakers, author talks, and the like, but the main reason to attend is to visit publishers' booths to find out about upcoming titles and trends in publishing. ComicCon can be an excellent stop for librarians who have healthy graphic novel collections or who circulate comic books, but it is more than just comics—ComicCon is a pop-culture convention, featuring all kinds of media: television, movies, and online. Often cult or science fiction shows like *Lost*, *Heroes*, or *Battlestar Galactica* will send actors, writers, and directors to ComicCon to answer audience questions about their upcoming seasons and promote their shows. You will find a colorful cast of characters at ComicCon—because this is a general-interest trade show and not a library conference, many members of the public attend, and many of them do so in costume. Be sure to check the ComicCon website for information about special events, as they can be a lot of fun.

NETWORKING/GETTING INVOLVED

Beyond attending conferences, which in and of itself can be an excellent way to meet other librarians and learn, you may also be interested in taking a more active role in library organizations. Fortunately, it is not difficult to do this. Unfortunately, getting involved on this level can often be overwhelming and intimidating if you are new to librarianship, your area, or organizational participation. In talking with other teen librarians, I have heard many of them echo my feelings upon first becoming involved with YALSA: if you don't already know anyone, it feels like you're an outsider trying to break into a clique. Of course, YALSA members and YALSA leadership are disappointed to hear this, as it's their last intention to make anyone feel excluded, but it is a reality for some. There are ways of taking small steps to involvement, and once you have started to meet people and get the lay of the land, you will find it easier to participate. The same scenario may not be true of all library organizations, but rest assured that no matter what, it is OK to feel like taking it slowly when getting involved. Even the library rock stars had to start somewhere.

Library School Networking

Don't forget all those amazing people you just finished taking classes with! (Or, in some cases, knew ages ago but maybe still keep in touch with.) Do you have one professor whom you can reach out to? Not all professors are active in library organizations, but they could point you in the right direction and make introductions. Or, perhaps your library school has volunteer opportunities for graduates—mentoring programs, for example, or monthly discussions.

Additionally, your fellow classmates may have ideas for you. Some of my colleagues who went to Pratt have friends who graduated with them who are now working in library publishing, an avenue that not many of us think of or pursue when graduating from library school. Library publishing includes trade journals, database vendors, and the library marketing groups of major publishers. Librarians who work in the private sector will offer you a fresh perspective on the field. They may be more tapped into tech trends or publishing trends, and they may be able to keep you abreast of big events coming up. Even if you are not job hunting, it is always a good idea to nurture the relationships you have with others in the field. You never know when someone might be able to offer you a cool opportunity to try something new, let you know about an amazing job opening, or even just invite you out to dinner with other exciting librarians.

Committee Work

Joining a committee at the national level can be extremely satisfying, but can also be time consuming and require travel to conferences. YALSA has changed its requirements for conference attendance for committee members so that all process committee members are virtual members, meaning they do not have to travel to conferences. But this is not the case for selection committees and some other groups (read on for more information about the differences between these two types of committees). You will also find many ways of getting involved in state and local library organizations, which can often allow you to have more responsibilities than you would on the national level and can be excellent ways to gain experience and to network. For specific information about YALSA committees, visit http://www.ala.org/ala/mgrps/divs/yalsa/getinvolved/participate.cfm.

When it comes to YALSA, there are two types of committee: the process committee and the selection committee. Many consider selection committees to be prestigious appointments, because often their work leads to an award being given—and often these awards receive press attention. Additionally, the work of process committees remains in the ALA records, as their lists and awards are kept on record. Some of YALSA's selection committees include:

- Best Fiction for Young Adults
- Michael L. Printz Award

- Alex Awards
- Margaret A. Edwards Award
- Quick Picks for Young Adults

Because selection committees are in high demand, they can be difficult to be appointed to. You may need to have experience doing other work for YALSA in order to be considered—the appointing committee will want to see a record of responsible work in some area within YALSA. And you should also know that it can take an enormous amount of time to be active on a selection committee, as you will be reading or listening to or viewing dozens—if not hundreds—of books or videos. In most cases, publishers send copies of books, usually ARCs, to committee members, who are expected to read them in order to consider them for an award or selection list. Each selection committee has a chair, who is appointed by the YALSA selection committee.

YALSA's process committees are equally time and labor intensive, but in a different way. Process committees are expected to work toward a particular outcome. Some are based on an annual project, like the Teen Tech Week committee, while others have ongoing duties and can outline their own goals. These committees do much of their work virtually, and each one has a chair, who, in my experience, spends even more time working on these projects. The chair must keep the rest of the group focused and on track and is responsible for communicating information back ad forth between the members and YALSA leadership. Committee chairs are often asked to present information to the YALSA board at annual meetings and have to write reports of their activities. Examples of some of the process committees available are:

- Teen Tech Week
- Teens' Top Ten
- Organization and Bylaws
- Editorial Advisory Board
- Strategic Planning

As a librarian starting out, if you are able to visit ALA conferences, stop by the YALSA all-committee meeting, usually held on Saturday morning. You will be able to sit in on different committee meetings and meet YALSA members who are involved on different levels. Every winter, YALSA puts out a call for volunteers to sit on different committees; that is your chance to apply for any committees that look interesting to you. If you apply for a few, you may be appointed to one of them. You may wish to speak with involved YALSA members about which groups are actively seeking new members or that are easier to be appointed to before you fill out your application, too. Just don't forget that you may have an obligation to attend both ALA meetings, which could be an issue to discuss with your administration before accepting any offers.

Proposals for Speaking and Writing

Having your name in print or speaking at a conference or meeting of any kind is excellent for your résumé. It sets you apart from your peers and suggests that you might be considered an expert in a particular area. That said, it can be very difficult to do both, and often your chance of having a proposal accepted depends on the connections you have made—which is another reason why it's a good idea to meet and get to know as many fellow librarians as you can. There are a few resources available for those who are interested in speaking or writing. Like anything else, it gets easier the more you do it. As your résumé grows, so will your visibility and your chances of being asked to speak or write.

Keep on top of these two blogs, which feature speaking and writing opportunities:

- *Beyond the Job:* http://www.beyondthejob.org
- *A Library Writer's Blog:* http://librarywriting.blogspot.com

In addition, searching for *call for proposals* and *library* in any search engine will lead you to numerous websites asking for writing and speaking proposals, many put out by state library associations.

When you are ready to write up a proposal, keep a few questions in mind:

- Is your idea unique, new, or does it fit a niche? Are there already tons of books, articles, and research about this topic, or are you one of the first to touch on it?
- Can you offer a fresh perspective on a staid topic? Can you show people how to do something in a new way or shake up a traditional method?
- Do you have research or experience to back up your claims? Can you show people the result of your work? Is there an outcome that could be of interest to other librarians?

- Will your ideas be useful for others in the field? Can you offer practical advice or theories that could be interpreted and used by others?
- Do you have experience or a publishing history that demonstrates your authority in this area?

There are a few ways to brainstorm ideas for such a proposal:

- Look at the major projects that you have undertaken in your time at the library. Evaluate them to see if you have done anything that might be considered innovative. Look at your most successful projects and examine the outcomes.
- Think about trends in librarianship and pay attention to what other librarians are writing or speaking about. Identify three trends and think about how your experiences fall into those trends. For example, if you have created an amazing podcasting program, perhaps you could tie that to the idea of youth participation, integrating user-generated content into programming, or promoting creative media with teens.
- Write about what you know. Don't try to come up with a crazy new theory or guess about what might work. Write about your program and your experiences. If you can get your teens involved, all the better—see if they can be interviewed via Skype, or ask if you can show off their work.

Submitting a writing proposal can be as simple as sending in an already-written article or as complicated as writing up a lengthy proposal as outlined by the publisher. Applications for speaking engagements often have forms for you to fill out. Visit the websites of major magazines to see their proposal guidelines, and visit the sites of conferences to find the same for speaking proposals. Be clear and concise, and keep true to your voice. One way to get started is to co-write or co-present, either with a colleague or someone you know in the field. It can take some of the pressure off you and even offer a new perspective to those who are reviewing proposals. If you have few credentials, it might help to partner with someone who is a bit more seasoned or who can boast of a few writing or presenting credits.

Additionally, smaller conferences and publications are the best place to start. Look at state library conferences and smaller magazines or newsletters—or blogs—before you send things off to *School Library Journal* and *Internet Librarian*. If you have your own blog, keep it active and make sure people know about it. Send your blog updates to Twitter and promote your blog any way you can (can you put it in your e-mail signature? On a MOO mini business card?). Even if no one is reading it, when you write up your proposal and include a link to your blog, editors will be able to visit it to check out your writing and your ideas.

CAREER GROWTH: WHERE DO YOU GO FROM HERE?

Chances are, you will spend much time—a year and more—just getting your bearings, planning, and developing. During that time, you won't be thinking much about career growth, probably. But it may come up eventually, and if you want to move up in your organization—or in any organization—you will start thinking about the next steps in your career.

Building Your Résumé

While I don't recommend thinking of your résumé first and your services second, it's always good to be aware of opportunities to add skills and accomplishments to your résumé. You will do this naturally as you complete the responsibilities of your job, and as you get involved in professional development opportunities. But there are other ways of building your résumé or curriculum vitae (CV). At work, if there is a new project that you can take on or an initiative that you can spearhead, you will not only be learning and giving yourself the chance to shine in your library, you will also be adding to your skills as a librarian.

When it comes to your career growth, think about where you want to be in five and 10 years. Do you want to head up a large department? Do you want to move up the ladder in management and eventually become an assistant director? Do you want to work for an overseeing body? Once you have thought about this, you can try to chart out a course for yourself within the organization. What skills are necessary for that kind of leadership? Or, if you would like to stay a front-line staff member, how can you get better? Here are some tips:

- Be visible. Spend time in other areas of the library, just saying hello to your colleagues. Offer to help out on other desks. Walk around when you have a bit of free time. The better known you are, the more advocates you will have. This won't help you with your résumé, but it will help you develop connections in the organization, which can lead to more opportunities. Meet with your superiors as often as you can—set up a regular meeting with them—and report to them on what you're working on, what you're planning, and what you need help with.

- Be involved. While I can't advocate for saying yes to everything, I do think that at the beginning of your career it's important to show that you are a team player and that you welcome new challenges. If a big project is underway or a new group is being formed, either volunteer to be on it, or say yes when someone asks you to be. You will connect with staff members you might normally work with, and you will learn from the experience. At the same time, think about ways to be involved outside of your library. Can you join a local roundtable or a state committee? This sort of activity is another way of showing that you are interested in expanding your skill set and that you are committed to librarianship.

- Keep educating yourself. Partaking in continuing education opportunities is not only good for becoming a better librarian, it shows your management that you care about your field and your library. Attendance at these events can go on your résumé, and such events will connect you with other librarians who may be interested in collaborating with you later on.

- Make a name for yourself. Whether it's on a local scale or a larger one, find a way to set yourself apart. This might be through actively seeking speaking engagements, submitting writing proposals, blogging, or setting up a website. If you have a particular message that you want to make your brand, all the better. While this can be a long process, some of the most successful librarians I know have an issue—or two—that they consistently advocate for, speak about, and write about. This allows them to create an identity for themselves within the library sphere. For a teen librarian, these issues might be youth participation, integrating technology, mobile technology, school collaboration, media literacy, or any number of important issues. Take some time to think about what you love and are most interested in in the field, and be genuine—find something you really care about, not something you think will be the most unique or trendy.

- Keep track of your accomplishments. As you complete major projects, keep a note of that somewhere. If you write an annual or monthly report, make sure you are also including that information somewhere in your personal files. Keep track of statistics that you improved and other quantifiable indicators of your success, as well as anecdotes and quality improvements.

STRESS AND TIME MANAGEMENT

I have met a lot of very special librarians in my day. All of them have one thing in common: they work very, very hard. In a field where things are constantly changing and the profession's reputation seems constantly at stake, committed librarians are pushing themselves as hard as they can. Especially if you are developing a new program—and on your own, no less—you may find yourself burning out. We no longer work in a 40-hour-a-week world, union shop or not. Smart phones and laptops make it very difficult to unplug when we get home, and the increasing demands of your position on top of hours on public service desks mean you may not be able to fit everything into your set work hours. I have never worked at an organization where I have completely shut off at the end of the day.

The world of libraries can be fairly insular, and it can be easy to forget about the outside world. Work hard, certainly—it will lead to good things professionally, and it will give you great pride in what you do—but make your outside-of-work life a priority, too.

There are few ways you can try to prevent excess stress and burnout, and there are also many books and articles written on the topic. Here's my advice.

Time management

- Keep a to-do list. This can be anything from a paper list that you check at the start of every day and cross off as you go, or a lot of sticky notes up on your wall, or it can involve software that travels with you. I have used both Evernote (http://evernote.com) and ToodleDo (http://www.toodledo.com) in the past; I prefer Evernote because I can keep other notes and information all in one place; for example, I have conference notes, meeting notes, ideas, and my to-do list all in my account, which I can then access from any computer *and* my phone.

- Prioritize. My former director had a great way of putting it: on every to-do list, there are A items (the most important), B items, and C items. Most people can't handle those A items—they are too complex or time consuming—so they focus on the B and C items instead. That means that those big, important A items never get addressed. This can mean that you're ignoring the most crucial parts of your job. There are a couple of ways to handle this. One, break down your A items into manageable tasks. So, say you have to plan a big event. Don't write down "plan end-of-summer party." Write down all the little things that need to get done to make that happen: making invitations, buying refreshments, booking a musical act, and the like. If you need help prioritizing, ask your manager what she thinks you should be working on first. Especially if you're in a new work environment, you may not know what the expectations are. If you've got a bunch of things on your list that all seem really important, your boss will be able to help you get them in the right order.

- Do not be afraid to delegate. This can be difficult for overachievers or for anyone who's excited to be getting some real professional responsibilities. Why hand away your job to someone else? What if you don't get the credit? You will need to let that go if you're finding yourself unable to do all that is required of you within a reasonable time. There are certain tasks that do not need to be done by you. Can you have volunteers help put spine labels on books, or ask teens to be in charge of calling local businesses to ask for food donations? Sometimes there are good reasons to do these things that don't just involve time management! Don't fret about credit—if you are the one designing and managing a project, people will know. Asking for help with the little things means you will have more time and energy to focus on the big picture.

Stress

- If you can, unplug. If you have been given a laptop or smart phone by your boss with the expectation that you will be using it to work from home, be clear about those expectations. Are you expected to be on call 24/7, or is it really only for travel and emergencies? How long does your e-mail turnaround time need to be? If you work in a school, there are often guidelines for how quickly you must respond to parents, though usually it is within 24 hours—which means you can wait till the next morning if you get an e-mail at night. The more you take on, the harder it can be to turn off your phone or your computer, but it's *crucial* that you do it when you can. No matter what your personal situation is—married, single, living at home, parenting—you deserve time away from work.

- Learn how to say no. This is nearly impossible for me, especially when it comes to outside-of-work opportunities like writing or presenting. But you have to be realistic. If you are in the middle of a big project, it's not the time to take on an assignment that will require hours of work every night when you get home. Committee work can also be extremely time consuming. It is better to say no than to start missing deadlines or letting down team members. That said, if an opportunity comes along that you can't pass up, see if you can negotiate with the person offering it. Can you start a bit later than proposed? Can you share the opportunity with another librarian? At the same time, try not to take on too much at work. Focus on what's most important and try to limit the number of tasks you take on that are not directly related to your position. This can also be extremely difficult, as you will likely want to make connections, be a team player, and be known as a hard worker. But your colleagues will understand if you tell them that you would like to get your feet underneath you before you join a task force or help plan the holiday party.

- Talk to people. Talk to your boss, your coworkers, and people in other departments. Be friendly, be honest, and avoid gossip. Don't keep stress a secret. If something is truly bothering you, your boss needs to know. Don't go to a work friend to complain and blow off steam—it could come back to bite you. But if you need advice, sometimes a trusted colleague can be a good person to approach. Be professional and thoughtful about your words, and you'll be fine.

- Focus on your life outside of work. Nothing helps more with work stress than finding and doing something you enjoy outside of work. Whether it's yoga, brewing your own beer, knitting, or walking your dog, find something that doesn't have anything to do with work and make it a priority. This is what will get you through tough days. It can be such a challenge to turn off your brain to work, even when you're not in the building, but going to salsa class or digging in your garden can certainly help.

I am proud to be part of a profession that is constantly reinventing itself, forcing its members to stay on their toes and turn on a dime. It's an exciting time to be a librarian. Our traditional roles are being challenged—and though it can be sometimes scary, it's a powerful feeling, knowing that we have the opportunity to change the public's perception of us. Teens deserve librarians who push the limits, take on new challenges, and meet adversity head on. Perhaps more than those who serve other populations, teen librarians must be nimble and open-minded—teens' interests and needs can change more quickly than we could ever imagine. If we're going to develop successful teen programs, we have to be ready to change, too. Fortunately, there is a supportive, forward-thinking community of librarians at the ready to welcome you into the fold, to teach you new skills, and to put tools directly into your hands. We are very lucky to have such a powerful support system, because we need it: libraries are closing, and schools are laying off media specialists. If we're going to stay viable, we're going to have to fight for it. Be proud that you have made this choice not only to be a librarian, but to be a librarian serving teens. You are entering the field in a day and age when you can make a significant difference in a teen's life. And to counter the bad news about libraries is a whole lot of good news—amazing things are happening. You're a part of that. So I leave you with this: good luck. Best wishes. Have fun. And bravo!

INDEX

Administration, 19–21, 37, 112, 155, 192
Adult collection, 41–42, 55, 64
Advocacy, 14–15, 75, 160, 168; gaming, 110
Age restriction, 34
American Library Association, 6, 9, 74–75, 168–69, 172, 174, 180, 183–84; conferences, 186, 191–92

Booklists, 13, 44–46, 54–55, 102, 123, 173–74
Books: awards, 55–57, 173, 190–91; blogs, 57; reviews, 58
Book talking, 133–34
Book trailers, 77, 92, 179
Budget, 63–64, 69–71, 76, 91, 102, 106–9, 117, 119, 149–69
Bullying, 32, 33, 35, 111, 122–23

Children, 10–11, 22, 34, 96, 111, 172
Children's books, 42–43, 58–59
Collection challenges, 41, 72–75, 109–11

Community partnerships, 14, 137–40, 143
Community service, 92, 100, 114, 135, 137–38
Computer games, 87–90, 92
Computers, 10, 64–65
Conferences, 172, 174, 183, 184, 185–89, 193
Crafts, 94
Cyberbullying, 35–37

Databases, 13, 44–45, 64, 65, 97, 135–36, 151
Décor, 29–31, 108
Displays, 25, 27, 30, 31, 66–68, 102

E-mail outreach, 99, 133, 135, 141, 144

Facebook, 93, 114, 125, 126–28, 129, 133, 141, 142, 145–46, 168, 181
Filtering, 33–35
Focus groups, 59, 168
Furniture, 30–31, 151

Gaming, 82–91; consoles, 84–86; furniture, 30; handhelds, 87; programming, 82–83, 109–11; reviewing, 48, 83–84
Genres, 43, 45–46, 53–54, 68
Grants, 164–65, 172, 180
Graphic novels, 43, 45, 55, 56, 62–63, 75, 79

Homework: collections, 59, 63–65; supporting, 10, 13, 30, 96, 107, 116, 156
Honor baskets, 76

Information literacy, 13, 110–11
Instant messaging, 131

Job hunting, 6–8

Library board, 24, 73, 109, 112
Library websites, 19, 24, 36, 96, 105, 119
Listservs, 174, 179–80, 185

Magazine collection, 41, 71
Materials requests, 69, 164
Mission statements, 17–18, 40
Movies, 48–52, 85, 86
Music, 52–53, 93, 100

Networking, 138–39, 171, 173, 184, 186, 189–90
Nonfiction, 43, 44, 56, 59, 62, 63–64, 65

Older teens, 63, 65, 115

Parents, 24, 33, 51, 78, 82, 85, 95–96, 99, 102, 105, 111, 126, 138–39, 140–41
Policies, 18–19; behavior 32–33, 36; collection development and circulation, 39–41, 47, 72
Press releases, 99, 118, 131, 140–41, 143

Professional committees, 186, 190–92, 195, 197
Publicity, 26, 103, 105, 111, 140–43; design 94, 116, 118, 123–25

Reader's advisory, 44, 54, 60, 133, 173
Reluctant readers, 59, 60–63
Resumes, 5, 182, 184, 18,7, 192, 194–95
Review journals; 54, 174

School libraries, 13, 21–22, 24, 41, 44, 63, 64, 76, 97, 114, 131–32, 133, 135, 143, 171
School visits, 134–35, 136–37, 141
Scratch, 92
Statistics, 43, 69, 106, 146, 152–54, 168, 195
Summer reading, 98–102, 133, 138, 144, 163
Supplies, 25, 27, 93, 108, 117, 150, 168

Teachers, 29, 41, 59, 64, 97, 99, 131–33, 135, 136–37, 143–44
Technology, 6, 7, 10, 12, 91–93, 118–19
Teen committees, 118–19
Teen development, 10–11, 14, 23–24
Teen space, 29–33, 64–65, 125, 175
Text messaging, 35, 37, 92, 129–31, 141
Theft, 32, 75–76, 91
Twitter, 125, 128, 133, 141, 142, 145, 178–79, 180–81, 193

Volunteers, 24–26, 138, 197

Webinars, 174, 180, 183, 184, 185

Young Adult Library Services Association, 9, 14, 15, 23–24, 51, 54–56, 67, 69, 75, 107, 165, 168, 172, 173–74, 177, 179–80, 181, 186, 187, 189, 190–92
Youth groups, 114, 137–38
Youth participation, 23–24, 193, 195

ABOUT THE AUTHOR

SARAH LUDWIG is the academic technology coordinator at Hamden Hall Country Day School in Hamden, Connecticut. Formerly, she was head of teen and technology services and head of knowledge and learning services at Darien Library in Darien, Connecticut. She received her MLS from Simmons College. She is a regular contributor to the *Young Adult Library Services Association* blog and the "Tag Team Tech" column in *VOYA*. In 2010, Ludwig was selected as an American Library Association Emerging Leader.